5 SIMPLE STEPS TO TAKE YOUR MARRIAGE
FROM GOOD TO GREAT

SIMPLE 5 STEPS

TO TAKE YOUR MARRIAGE

FROM

GOOD TO GREAT

Terri L. Orbuch, Ph.D.

DELACORTE PRESS

Published in the United States by Delacorte Press, an imprint of The Random House Publishing Group, a division of Random House, Inc., New York.

DELACORTE PRESS is a registered trademark of Random House, Inc., and the colophon is a trademark of Random House, Inc.

Library of Congress Cataloging-in-Publication Data
Orbuch, Terri.
5 simple steps to take your marriage from good to great / Terri L. Orbuch.
p. cm.
Includes bibliographical references.
ISBN 978-0-385-34286-5
1. Marriage—Psychological aspects. 2. Communication in marriage.
I. Title. II. Title: Five simple steps to take your marriage from good to great.
HQ734.O68 2009
646.7'8—dc22   2009029292

Printed in the United States of America on acid-free paper

www.bantamdell.com

2 4 6 8 9 7 5 3 1

FIRST EDITION

Book design by Casey Hampton

*To my husband, Stuart—with each year
our marriage grows more wonderful*

To my parents, Joyce and Marty—who truly have a great marriage

CONTENTS

ACKNOWLEDGMENTS

There are many people whose assistance and support have made this book possible. First and foremost, I would like to thank all of the participants in the Early Years of Marriage (EYM) project. Without your continued involvement and dedication, the research study and book would not be possible.

Also, there are some people you meet, who you know are special and who instantly become a part of your life. It was like that with my colleague and friend Joe Veroff whose initial vision drove the EYM project. His guidance, mentorship, and friendship will always be a lasting memory and source of joy for me. Both Joe and John Harvey taught me never to be afraid to go beyond the boundaries of academic scholarship. Thank you!

I am grateful to all of the students and colleagues who worked passionately on the EYM project over the last twenty-two years, such as Elizabeth Douvan, Shirley Hatchett, Edna Brown, Linda Acitelli, Toni Antonucci, Hiroko Akiyama, Halimah Hassan, Diane Holmberg, Sandra Eyster, Lindsay Custer, Michele Acker, Jose Bauermeister, Cara Talaska, Charlea McNeal, Laura Hagan, Kira Birditt, Lisa Byrd, and the many Survey Research Center field interviewers and staff. Together we have gained important knowledge about what keeps marriages together and what breaks them apart. In addition, I am appreciative of the financial support provided by the National Institutes of Health.

I also want to thank Gail Bradney, whose insight, intelligence, and transformational writing skills helped me tremendously. What an adventure it's been! I appreciate the enthusiasm and perseverance of my agent, Jill Marsal, and my public relations consultants—Cathy Lewis, Carolyn Krieger-Cohen, and Nancy Rosen. Thank you to my incredible editor Danielle Perez at Bantam Dell, who was committed to this project from the beginning and assisted me in many ways throughout the entire process, and to Susan Corcoran, Katie Rudkin, and Quinne Rogers at Bantam Dell.

And most important, my personal relationships that mean the world to me. My husband, whose love, support, and partnership have helped my dreams become reality. To my children, thank you for your kisses, hugs, and patience while I spent many hours on the computer. I am so proud of you both! To my sister, brother, and good friends, thank you for your valued friendship and love. And to my parents, who taught me early on about love, to ask questions, to have confidence in myself, and to value relationships.

CAVEAT: A NOTE TO READERS

This book is written and designed for husbands and wives who love each other, but feel their marriages could be better. These strategies are time-tested and extremely effective for couples who define their marriages as "decent" or "good." However, if you are experiencing problems in your marriage that stem from serious, deep-rooted issues, such as substance abuse or mental illness, this book may not provide enough support. Moreover, if you are currently in a seriously troubled marriage characterized by chronic physical or psychological abuse, constant criticism, or pervasive contempt, this book may not give you the help you seek. If you are feeling hopeless and helpless in your marriage, and especially if you are feeling frightened or threatened, I would urge you to seek professional help from your pastor or rabbi, a marriage counselor or therapist, or your county mental health agency. There's always hope for happiness, and you deserve to be happy.

INTRODUCTION

In and around the greater metropolitan area of Detroit, where I have a private practice as a marriage and family therapist, teach university students, and direct a landmark government-funded, long-term research study of marriage, I am known as Dr. Terri Orbuch—a psychologist, sociologist, professor, and relationship researcher.

But outside of my counseling office and the ivory towers of the two Michigan universities where I work—Oakland University and University of Michigan—I am known as The Love Doctor®, a nationally recognized relationship adviser who has been on television and radio, in print, and online. I have a reputation for being optimistic and nonjudgmental, and people say they love my concrete, helpful tips that they can apply right away to make their relationships healthier and more fulfilling. I listen to questions about love, dating, sex, marriage, and all kinds of relationships, and then offer advice that's upbeat, easy to use, and based on science.

TURNING SCIENTIFIC RESEARCH INTO TIPS YOU CAN USE

Why does someone from the world of academia put herself out there like this? It's because I had an epiphany a few years ago while poring over fascinating data on marriage and reading the latest findings in relationship research. It was this: Very few of the people who can really *use* great information about marriage and relationships ever get to see, learn about, and benefit from the findings of my research and that of other relationship scientists. That's because most of the really good relationship research gets published only in academic journals and papers, which are not accessible to the general public without a subscription or university affiliation.

Unless one suffers from insomnia, who in their right mind wants to pick up an academic journal full of jargon-laden research findings and statistics to try to get some helpful information? Let me give you an example so you will see what I mean. In one of my recent academic journal articles, I wrote about the effects of wives' education on the stability of marriages over the first fourteen years of marriage:

Results indicate that the level of wives' education was significantly predictive of the risk of divorce. The odds of

divorce decrease by a factor of .76 for each additional year
of wives' schooling. . . . Education may give women the
resources and coping abilities to maintain and adapt to
transitions in their marriages.

It's a real page-turner, right? And yet, there's a nugget of wisdom here that could easily get lost in such dry academic language. I would translate these interesting findings into the
following: *Highly educated women are good for marriages.*
Despite what you may hear about women's education being
harmful to keeping marriages together, the reality is that in
my long-term study of marriage, the likelihood of divorce *decreased* by 24 percent for every additional year of education the
wife obtained. Education gives women information about the
realities of marriage, opportunities to develop coping skills in
response to stress, and people to turn to when they have concerns in their marriage.

It's a shame that such great information is read by only a
few, because many of these findings are groundbreaking and
potentially life-changing. My own husband of sixteen years
has gotten used to my quirky hobby of turning academic research into user-friendly tips. "Honey, guess what?" is how I
usually begin the conversation. He'll turn to me with The
Look. It's the "Okay, what are we trying *this* month?" look. I
have gotten him to try everything from riding a roller coaster
with me to spending an "unplugged" evening together with
our two teens—no lights, TV, music, or computers. My dar-
ling husband is a real sport! I would describe our marriage as
great, but with all the typical issues of division of labor,

compromise, busy schedules, and communication that other happy couples endure. One thing I have learned over the years is that scientific research is quite valuable when we give it practical applications. From my own marriage experience, and from observing hundreds of couples in my research, private practice, and workshops, I know that the science-based strategies and tips I've developed and use myself *really do work*.

Unlike many of my peers, I wanted to become a new kind of academician—a Ph.D. who could bring science to real couples in the form of highly practical tips and easy-to-understand approaches. I have a desire to make science accessible, understandable, and helpful to the general public. As The Love Doctor, I have been able to help people learn and apply new concepts and behaviors to make their marriages happier. This book brings together the latest scientific findings from my long-term study and findings from other relationship researchers to give you fresh insights, strategies, and ideas about marriage.

FOCUSING ON THE POSITIVE MAKES GOOD MARRIAGES GREAT

Perhaps the most common complaint I hear is: "Does marriage have to be such hard work?" If there's one message I hope to get across in this book, it's a resounding NO. I will show you how to create positive and significant changes in your marriage *instantly* by using well-researched, targeted actions and behaviors that work every time. And the best news is that you can make these changes yourself, without the assistance of a counselor or therapist!

Surprisingly, when we look at happy couples, we see that really great marriages are not the result of long hours of tedious hard work. In fact, it's actually small changes in behavior and attitude that create happiness over time. This is amazing news for couples who want to make their marriages better, but who falsely believe the journey will be long, arduous, complicated, and filled with land mines.

My research shows that most marriages start with a good foundation that erodes over time, making it necessary for spouses to learn and implement simple changes to support and strengthen their marriage. A mistake many couples make—as do many couples therapists, I might add—is that they focus on the negative. What's wrong with the marriage, they ask? How can we fix it? My years of therapeutic experience and scientific observation have led me to conclude that a very different—and perhaps opposite—approach works better. I have found that the most effective way to boost happiness, commitment, harmony, fun, and passion in a marriage that is basically sound is to add new elements to the marriage, and focus on how to support and strengthen what's already working pretty well. To use a medical analogy, it would be similar to a physical therapist prescribing exercises to a patient suffering from back pain. If you take action to strengthen the parts that are working so they can support the weaker parts, rather than just treating the pain, real healing accelerates, and a positive, often permanent change in the underlying condition occurs. I strongly believe that introducing new, positive elements into the marriage is a much better way to produce change than long hours of problem-oriented therapy and analysis.

From observing hundreds of spouses over many years, I have concluded that good marriages are a lot like start-up businesses that grow into successful Fortune 500 companies. The ones that last and prosper follow certain patterns of behavior and share certain traits. Drawing from time-tested evidence of what works in happy marriages, I have developed five simple steps to take your marriage from good to great. I have successfully used these simple strategies in my practice as a family and marriage therapist and taught them in my marriage enrichment workshops. Couples at every stage of marriage have benefited from them. These strategies work because they are based on the best combination of sound research, common sense, and experience. They also work because they are unexpectedly quick and surprisingly simple.

It's a fact that couples face daunting obstacles during the early years of marriage. They run into roadblocks about such issues as whether to merge finances, how to manage work schedules, what friends to spend time with, and whether or when to have children. Census data report that nearly half of first marriages end in divorce—most of them in the first three to five years. Despite this, I have observed many highly successful couples grow stronger each year they are married. No matter what stage of marriage you are in, I am confident you and your spouse will benefit from learning these secrets to achieving marital happiness. These are behaviors and actions that have been proven to work time after time, with all kinds of couples, in all sorts of marriages.

BEING PART OF A HAPPY COUPLE

Do you remember the feeling of first being in love, when troubles and worries seemed to roll off your back and daily life was full of promise, sparkle, and excitement? Or can you recall a time when you were paralyzed by anxiety over a problem that seemed overwhelming, and your spouse not only listened to your fears and panic, but then came up with a solution that completely saved the day? These are the moments when your relationship serves as a safe haven and wonderful refuge, and as part of a happy couple, you feel an exquisite sense of gratitude, hope, and serenity about your future that's almost impossible for others to imagine.

You already know intuitively that being in a happy marriage is really good for you. That's because love and relationships are the backbone of our existence as human beings. Scores of scientific studies also confirm that happy relationships have profound effects on our physical and mental health. When we are in happy, loving relationships, we are better able to handle stress, more likely to be physically active, less likely to be depressed and suffer from illnesses, and in general, we live longer and healthier lives. In fact, studies show that people without happy relationships in their lives are two to five times more likely to get sick and die—during any nine-month period in which they are studied—than those who have a sense of interpersonal closeness in their lives.

But what makes couples happy? What makes marriages last? Is it possible for a so-so marriage to become a great one? As director of the only large-scale, long-term study of marriage in our country, the Early Years of Marriage project (EYM), funded by the National Institutes of Health (NIH), I have found the answers to these questions. After observing the same 373 couples over the course of more than twenty-two years, I am sitting on a gold mine of information that has never before been made available to the public.

We now know, for example, what makes couples compatible, how happy couples stay resilient in the face of extreme challenges, and which specific behaviors erode happiness over time and inevitably lead to divorce. We have learned how external stressors, such as money, employment, and in-laws, affect happiness, and we know what role internal relationship factors, such as sexuality, conflict, and communication, play in marital longevity.

But until now, the findings from my NIH study have been seen by only a few students, government employees, and academics. The very people who could benefit most from it—real married people like you—have not had access to this invaluable information. As a longtime researcher of relationships and as a university professor, I have collected a wealth of dazzling discoveries about sexuality, human mating patterns, the neurochemistry of attraction and love, relationship longevity, and offbeat insights from behavioral science. As I mentioned, I am passionate about bringing the findings from my long-term study, along with other scientists' priceless relationship research, to couples in a form they can readily use to make their marriages happier and more fulfilling. Science, after all, should be fun, accessible, and beneficial to all of us.

BACKGROUND ON THE NIH STUDY

The Early Years of Marriage project, funded by the NIH, is unprecedented in its scope and depth. It is the only study to follow the same group of married couples for more than twenty-two years, and was initiated in 1986. Given the high rate of divorce in the United States, the study was designed to identify what keeps marriages together and happy, and what breaks marriages apart over time. Many researchers had studied marriage previously, but this project is the only study to:

- Follow married couples over such a long period of time (more than twenty-two years to date). The study begins right after couples are married.
- Collect information from both members of the couple separately *as well as* from the couple jointly.
- Follow both black and white married couples. Surprisingly, little research attention has been given to black marriages and the styles of interaction that occur within them. We thought that what keeps marriages together and happy might differ for black and white couples.
- Look at both external stressors (e.g., money, employment, in-laws) and internal relationship factors (e.g., sexuality, conflict, communication) for their effects on marriages over time.

When the project first received funding from the NIH, we proposed to follow the couples for only four years, which is why it is called the "Early Years of Marriage Project." But after catching a glimpse of how powerful the findings were, we decided to continue to follow the married couples. We never changed the title of the project, even though I would argue that the couples are now into their "Early Middle Years of Marriage," because we wanted the couples to easily recognize the project.

In the EYM study, the goal was to examine a large and diverse group of married couples. Previous research studies, which have followed married couples over time, had relied either on couples seeking marital counseling or on volunteers recruited through advertising. The problem with studying these groups is that couples in counseling are likely to be experiencing more marital problems than the average, whereas volunteers may be more secure with their relationships or want to get advice about specific problems in their marriages. From a scientist's perspective, we wanted to assemble a pool of study participants that would not have these influencing traits and would be more representative of typical American couples.

To obtain a broad group of couples, we turned to marriage licenses, which provide a complete list of all the couples preparing for marriage in a given area. Working with a county clerk's office in the Midwest, we obtained names and contact information for every couple who applied for a marriage license in that county within a three-month period in 1986. We then approached these couples and asked them to take part in the study.

The particular county we selected was a good one, because it allowed us to look at couples from all walks of life, from communities ranging from poor inner-city neighborhoods to posh suburban areas. Also, this county has a sizable black population. Although we would have liked to include couples of other races in this study (e.g., Asian, Hispanic, Native American), they are less common in this particular county. We were also interested in couples who were matched in their racial background. Although interracial couples would make for fascinating research, these couples have a different set of obstacles and challenges, which are beyond the scope of our study objectives.

We interviewed the couples at their homes on multiple occasions. Most couples were interviewed seven times—a few months after marriage (year one) and then at year two, three, four, seven, fourteen, and sixteen. We are planning on more face-to-face interviews at year twenty-five. The very first interview, shortly after the couple has married, represents a time when most couples are deeply immersed in the glow of the honeymoon period. In each subsequent interview, we added new relevant questions, but in general, the couples answered the same questions and did the same procedures each time they were interviewed. This allowed us to evaluate how specific sets of questions or topics (e.g., marital happiness, conflict, sexuality) change over the course of a marriage.

In order to capture the diversity and depth of marriages, we used two forms of data collection. First, we conducted face-to-face interviews with all the spouses using a comprehensive set of questions concerning their marriages.

Interviewing spouses separately was important, as spouses might feel less constrained about revealing certain aspects of their partner or marriage when interviewed alone than they would when interviewed together. In total, spouses answered close to two thousand questions on a variety of topics such as marital happiness, conflict, sexuality, children, family of origin, housework and child care, friends, leisure activities, religion, and employment experiences. We also conducted face-to-face interviews with each couple together where they were asked jointly to answer a variety of questions.

Next, because views of marriage are often complex and highly personal, we determined that interview data alone could not adequately capture the many nuances of couples' relationships. Accordingly, during each couple interview, we also asked spouses to do two unusual tasks together. One was a narrative procedure, asking them to tell the story of their relationship, from when they first met, became a couple, and got married, to their present relationship and projected future together. This procedure allowed participants to describe their marriages in their own words and tell detailed stories about their marriages and their spouses, and to identify the key issues in their relationships. The other task couples did together was to discuss the important rules for a really great marriage, during which we observed how they resolved their differences. Both of these procedures were novel and had not been used in other marriage research.

With meticulously assembled data from these two latter, more innovative procedures, I have been able to describe accurately and in detail what makes average couples happy or not in their marriages, and how couples who describe themselves as reasonably happy take their marriages from good to really great. Combining information from the narratives, behavioral observations, and the in-depth personal interviews has provided me with a wealth of data from which to speak confidently about how couples can move beyond a so-so marriage to one that is exceptional, robust, and enduring.

Every time we went back to interview the couples, we hired interviewers who then went through extensive training and preparation. As part of their training, they were instructed not to give couples advice or recommendations about marital issues or problems during the study. If couples asked for advice or suggestions, interviewers were equipped with a list of county clinics in the area, which they could leave with the spouses. It was critical not to change or affect the marriages we were studying. Couples were also told that they did not have to remember what they had said in the last interview nor worry about being repetitious.

We keep in contact with all of the couples by sending a project newsletter to them each summer. The newsletter keeps the couples updated on project news and information, although again we are careful not to give advice or tips about marriage or divorce. In the newsletter, they are also reminded about the importance of updating the project regarding changes in their marriages or families (like the birth of a child, divorce, moving to a new state), via a postcard (sent with the newsletter) or our project website.

The most common question I am asked about the study is: "What is the divorce rate?" It turns out that the divorce rate for this group of couples is identical to the national Census data statistics: Nearly half of all married couples who began the study in 1986 got a divorce (45 percent).

What happened to the couples who divorced over the last twenty-two years in terms of the study? If a couple divorced, both spouses continued to be interviewed. We asked divorced spouses a different comprehensive set of questions about their divorce, adjustment after divorce, and life at the present time. Essentially, at this point in the project I like to say that we have been following 746 married individuals for over twenty-two years since 1986—half of whom are still married to each other and half of whom were once married to each other.

The EYM project is still ongoing and has consistently been funded by the NIH. The study continues to reveal new and important findings about what keeps couples together and happy over the long term, and what breaks them apart.

THE FIVE STEPS TO A GREAT MARRIAGE

I got interested in writing this book after listening to the same questions and concerns again and again from my research couples, therapy patients, radio and TV audiences, workshop participants, and graduate students. Common themes I would hear include what to do when the passion wanes, how to deal with the marriage "blahs," when to worry about domestic bickering, how to handle spousal pet peeves, how to cope with growing apart, and how to survive a betrayal.

I soon recognized that it's not the big events that make couples unhappy but instead the seemingly minor everyday challenges. Most couples are elated, optimistic, and filled with overwhelming happiness at the beginning of their relationship. But over time the small and constant bumps in the road seem to wear down their happiness. Your partner doesn't notice you. Your partner doesn't listen. Your partner seems bored. You snap at each other. There are little squabbles. You get on each other's nerves.

It may surprise you to learn that deaths, major illnesses, or tragedies such as fire or bankruptcy are not the greatest causes of marital strife and struggle. Interestingly, in times of great hardship, spouses tend to lean on each other. When there is great stress coming from outside the marriage, most couples turn inward to their marriages for relief, love, and support. They frequently say tough times and life-changing challenges brought them closer together and made their bond stronger.

In this book, you'll learn the five strategies I developed that have been shown time and again to help couples navigate through the most common minefields of marriage. Following these five simple steps will help you take a marriage from mediocrity to greatness. You will learn to identify those parts of your marriage that need some extra support, and then add positive elements to your relationship to make it stronger, more exciting, happier, and even more profound. Why settle for a so-so marriage when you can propel it to one that is exceptional? Some of these steps may seem counterintuitive, but trust me—they really do work.

Step 1 is "Expect less, get more." In this eye-opening step, you will learn that the key to taking your marriage from good to really great is to neutralize the frustration that is slowly

THE COUPLES AT A GLANCE

We compared my NIH sample of married couples to two national samples: Census Data and the General Social Survey Data. When compared to these other samples, the married couples from my NIH study were consistent with national norms for first-married individuals by race—on income, education, parental status, likelihood of cohabitation, and a host of other demographic factors. I argue that the broadly representative makeup of this sample enhances the significance of the project findings.

WHO WAS ELIGIBLE: White (non-Hispanic) and black couples matched in their racial background who applied for marriage licenses in a Midwest county in 1986. Although other ethnicities (Asian, Hispanic, Native American) and mixed-ethnicity marriages make for fascinating research, we elected to exclude these groups because we would not have obtained sufficient numbers in this county to allow adequate statistical comparisons.

AGE: In year one, spouses were between twenty-five and thirty-seven years old.

EDUCATION: The average educational level included one year of postsecondary schooling, although some spouses did not finish high school and others were in graduate school.

EMPLOYMENT: More than 90 percent of the men and 67 percent of the women were employed outside the home.

CHILDREN BEFORE MARRIAGE: About 55 percent of the black couples and 22 percent of the white couples had children before marriage.

COHABITATION: About 65 percent of the black couples and 41 percent of the white couples had cohabited before marriage.

HOME MAKEUP: More than 45 percent of the couples shared their home with others, usually their children, but sometimes with other adults (parents, siblings, friends) as well.

eating away at your relationship. You do this by dramatically changing your expectations. We'll dispel the most common relationship myths that create unrealistic expectations within marriages, and you'll discover what your spouse expects of you and the marriage—and identify your own marriage expectations as well.

In Step 2, "Give incentives and rewards," I present research-based, quick-fix strategies to keep your partner feeling affirmed, happy, and supported. This step will teach you how to implement basic behaviors that make your partnership hum like a well-oiled machine, and keep you and your spouse happy and focused on the same objective: achieving and maintaining a great relationship.

Step 3, "Have daily briefings," will show you how to practice the Ten-Minute Rule to gain strategic insights about your spouse. You will learn how to get to know your partner again in order to anticipate problems before they arise, and instantly understand your spouse's perspective when they do. Couples who are intimately familiar with each other's emotional worlds and lives are better able to propel their relationships to greatness. In this step, you will pick up a number of unique communication strategies that enhance spousal harmony.

In Step 4, "Implement change," you will learn to take risks in order to reduce boredom and keep your love life fresh and exciting. Couples need to shake things up a bit and learn new behaviors together if they want their marriage to move from humdrum to fun and really amazing. This is the step where you will learn how to reignite the passion in your marriage and spice up your sex life. I liken the tools in this step to the business idea of "thinking outside the box." Keeping a marriage fresh sometimes requires surprising your partner and gently knocking him or her off balance. I will show you how to do it—and why it works so well.

Step 5 is "Keep costs low, benefits high." I will show you how to audit marriage behaviors to weed out the unprofitable ones. All marriages have highs and lows, but when costs go down and the benefits gain momentum, you can take your marriage from good to really great. For each of the top six costly behaviors I identify, you will learn a quick strategy backed by research that changes the outcome so you don't have to work so hard to enjoy your marriage.

I have peppered activities such as quizzes, exercises, self-assessments, and question guides throughout to make the strategies come alive. In each step you will also find lots of research-based tips, resources, statistics, studies, and entertaining trivia about marriage, love, and relationships.

Throughout the book, you will also discover what happy marriages look like, and how happy couples talk about and define their marriages. You will read the stories of remarkable couples from my NIH marriage study in which both spouses identified themselves as very satisfied, happy, and stable *every year they were interviewed*, over the course of about two decades. In these cases, both spouses reported being "very certain" that they will be together five years from now. Their stories are poignant, funny, tragic, familiar, and I hope ultimately inspiring.

You will see how typical couples from a range of backgrounds turned their mediocre relationships into first-class marriages using the very principles and practices I present in this book. These happy couples are just like you, but they have found a way to communicate, roll with the punches, deal with messy and difficult issues, endure hardships—and remain best friends and lovers.

Designed to be fun, illuminating, and, above all, easy to put into practice, this is a book I hope you will talk about, share, and use with your spouse to take your own marriage from good to really great.

5 SIMPLE STEPS TO TAKE YOUR MARRIAGE
FROM GOOD TO GREAT

1

EXPECT LESS, GET MORE

Neutralize frustrations
that are eroding your relationship.

One trait happy couples in my study share is that they have learned how to have realistic expectations of their spouses and marriages. To take your marriage from good to great, it's essential to transform unrealistic expectations—the ones that rarely get met and then cause you frustration, anger, sadness, hurt, and other negative emotions—into more realistic versions that *will* be met.

Contrary to popular belief, the biggest reason marriages fail is not conflict, lack of communication, or sexual incompatibility. **It's frustration.** The first step to achieving a truly great marriage is to defuse the frustration that is eating away at the love and happiness in your relationship. Frustration creates tension that builds and eventually explodes. Enough of these explosions and you've got a broken marriage. Where does this frustration come from? Unrealistic expectations! By having realistic expectations of love, men, women, and relationships in general, and then realistic *personal* expectations between you and your spouse specifically, you can dramatically improve your marriage.

In the first part of this chapter, we will look at the ten most common myths about marriage, and the reality behind each one. The simple act of dispelling myths that drive your expectations is a necessary step toward arriving at more realistic expectations and reducing marital tension. By learning what relationship research tells us about how men and women relate, behave, and think, you can approach your marriage with fresh, unbiased knowledge. Whenever I share the scientific research that debunks these common myths in my classes, therapy sessions, or workshops, people are always astounded to discover that what they've believed all along about the other gender, love, or marriage is just not supported by scientific facts and rigorous research. After you get rid of relationship expectations that are based on myths, rather than rooted in reality, you will see immediate, significant improvements in your marriage. I've seen this so many times, I no longer doubt it.

In the second part of the chapter, you will examine the specific expectations you and your spouse have of each other and your marriage. I present a number of exercises that will ask you to dig deep within *you* and ask yourself, "What are my top *personal* expectations for how my marriage should work?" I will help you identify your own personal expectations from a list of the sixteen most common personal expectations of married couples that came out of my long-term study. You and your spouse will discover what is most important to each of you in your ideal marriage. You will learn how to prevent disappointment by sharing your personal expectations with your spouse so that each of you has a clear understanding of what is important to the other. My own research shows that spouses who can identify each other's personal expectations experience greater happiness over time.

When one couple from my study, Timbra and Alan, were asked at year seven what advice they would give to other young newlyweds, their answer was very typical of many happy couples:

> TIMBRA: Know what your spouse wants and expects—
> and communicate that to each other. You can avoid a
> lot of fighting that way.
>
> ALAN: (*laughing*) I've known her since we were fourteen.
> You'd think I'd have a clue by now. But seriously, she's
> right. We really know what our limitations are and
> what each other's dreams and expectations are. The
> only surprises we have in our marriage are the good
> ones.

These two are typical of the happy couples in my study who have reasonable expectations of themselves, their spouses, and their relationships—and really "get" each other. My research continues to confirm that happy couples who have such reasonable expectations experience less frustration in their marriages, and more affection, closeness, respect, trust, passion, fun, and overall well-being and satisfaction than their peers. Sounds enticing, doesn't it?

HOW FRUSTRATION SABOTAGES MARITAL HAPPINESS

Frustration is tension that builds up until it eventually erupts into disappointment, anger, or unhappiness. Frustration occurs when our expectations aren't met; we think something *should* occur or unfold one way, and then it doesn't go as we planned.

Psychologists think of relationship expectations much like a play's script. Each of us is given a script early on in life for how we should act in relationships. And from this script, we also have very strong assumptions about how others should perform or respond to us. These "should" statements are relationship expectations. If our love partner meets our "should" statements or relationship expectations, then we are very happy. If he or she doesn't meet these expectations, we become frustrated.

Many of us have been taught by the media, friends, and family that our spouse should be everything to us. We learn that when two people find each other and get married, their lives should be forever intertwined. We expect our spouse to be our best friend, an excellent parent, a great lover, a good provider, a loving caregiver, a willing volunteer, physically fit, healthy, sensitive, generous, well-liked, open-minded, polite, intelligent, with similar interests, and happy to spend leisure time with us. Phew—and that's just for starters! No one can be all that, so we really need to learn to change our expectations. When such unrealistic expectations are not met, we will feel frustrated. Bottom line: Frustration takes the fun and passion out of your relationship, and can be very corrosive over time.

Instead, we need to have expectations that are realistic. Let me give you a concrete example so you can see how it works. A wife has had a run-in with her teenage son after he got home from school and is feeling as though she didn't handle it well. She wants her husband's input and reassurance, and she's also realized that the boy should hear from his father. The boy is holed up in his room, and she's seething. Here is her unrealistic expectation: that her husband will be *100 percent available to her* when he walks in the door, because she's done the heavy lifting, and now it's his turn. She's looking for superman. You can see what's coming, right? When her husband arrives home, maybe he's had his own rough day and needs *her* support, and is desperate for a few moments to unwind and decompress. His aloof behavior doesn't signal that he's unconcerned or uninvolved, but she interprets it that way and is infuriated and *frustrated* by his seeming lack of attention to her needs and those of the family. Now let's rewind her scenario starting from a *realistic* expectation: that he will be caring, responsive, and a good listener once she has given him the heads-up about the situation, asked him directly for his help, and the two of them have blocked out a mutually convenient half hour before dinner to discuss the situation together. By expecting less, she gets more. The *less* you expect—when those expectations are potentially excessive and unrealistic—the *more* satisfaction you will get out of your marriage.

John and Sue-Ellen, one of the happy couples in my study, are a good example of this. They talk a lot about eliminating unrealistic expectations when asked why they are happy in their marriage together.

John and Sue-Ellen are both doctors who first met in medical school. They were both academically driven and competitive with each other, and made good study partners. They married eight years after they met. Sue-Ellen quit her job once their first child was born. "When I used to fantasize about marrying John, I saw myself with a stethoscope in one hand and a pacifier in the other," she said. "I expected that we'd share parenting and I'd have a successful career too." The reality turned out differently. Although Sue-Ellen enjoyed being home with her son, she describes feelings of loss, guilt, and self-judgment. "I had invested so much time and money into medical school, and here I was, singing along with Elmo on *Sesame Street*. I think my dad, even with his traditional values, wondered what the hell I was doing with my life." It took several years for her to come to terms with the fact that she was a stay-at-home mom with an MD.

In one interview, John nods in agreement when Sue-Ellen says, "Don't expect that marriage or life is perfect. You need to understand that life is not a movie." Sue-Ellen, especially, had idealistic views of marriage and how their lives together would look. In the early years, those idealized expectations created a lot of frustration and disappointment. Eventually, she made peace with her life, and she and John could relax and really appreciate the sweet family and home they had created together. They have an extremely happy and stable marriage that has lasted nearly twenty years.

STOP BELIEVING THE MYTHS BEHIND UNREALISTIC EXPECTATIONS

It's not easy to let go of your general beliefs about relationships. Some of them have been ingrained in you since childhood. You've picked up impressions about love, relationships, and marriage from movies, TV, and romance novels. You've formed opinions by observing the ups and downs in the relationships of your parents, family, and friends. And you've probably learned a thing or two about love firsthand. You may have read self-help books and highlighted key passages that rang true. And if nothing else, you've gleaned tips from watching *Oprah* and reading advice columns. Without even realizing it, you cling to strong opinions you've acquired about love and marriage *that aren't necessarily supported by science.*

I always tell people they can do themselves a big favor by looking at the scientific facts. The reason is twofold. First, myth-based beliefs affect how we evaluate our marital experiences and our spouses. For example, if you really believe that passion never dies, but you're in year five of marriage and it's just not that exciting anymore, you might draw the conclusion that something is seriously wrong with your marriage. You might get angry at your spouse for not doing his or her part in making your relationship better. You might even feel frustrated or lonely as you compare your relationship to your best friend's marriage. She's squeezed up against her spouse at the restaurant as they share an inside joke together, while you sit next to your husband reading the menu in silence! But if you understand the truth behind the myth—that marriage "blahs" are typical and can be easily remedied—you can calmly say, "Hey, my marriage isn't in trouble. This is *normal*." As I say to my patients, knowledge is power. When you understand what's really going on in your relationship, you have the power to change it. Knowing research-based facts helps to ease the frustration, which in turn leads to being able to approach your relationship in a way that will bring more satisfaction and happiness in your marriage.

Second, myths may not only affect our perceptions, but also our behavior in relationships. Take conflict, for instance. Let's say you think fighting is harmful. If you fear conflict and the effect it may have on your relationship, you're more likely to clam up when things bother you. You may never tell your spouse what annoys or irritates you, like when he chews with his mouth open, or she won't stop talking about her friends. The next thing you know, you develop the habit of staying silent, and you get all bottled up, tense, and secretive about your feelings. Things will build up inside you until one day you're slamming pots and pans around in the kitchen, just steaming about the latest annoyance, and your spouse has no clue why you're behaving like this. The alternative: Change your expectation about fighting in marriage. Understand that some amount of conflict is normal in marital relationships, and figure out new ways to talk about your feelings without any fear. What a relief!

We are bombarded in the media with myths and misconceptions about love and marriage that are repeated as fact, but are unfortunately firmly rooted in fiction. In contrast, research that is conducted with large, diverse groups of people on relationships is much more valid. Don't forget that the average experience of the average person depicts most of us and our marriage and love concerns. However, as you read the research findings in this book, don't worry if you don't fit the norm or average. It is simply a law of science that big generalizations from reputable research studies only apply to about 90 or 95 percent of us at any one time. There are no true "universal laws" about relationships that fit all of the people, all of the time. So sometimes you'll have an "aha" moment and a finding will really ring true to your own situation, but other times you may think, "Wow, that doesn't represent *me* at all." As you read the research, stay open-minded, figure out where you fit, and remember that we all have different families, backgrounds, and values—and these shape our marital experiences in unique ways.

You can reduce the frustration that may be sabotaging your marriage by examining which of your expectations about the opposite sex, love, and relationships are based on myths—and are therefore unrealistic—and which ones jibe with scientific research findings. Here's a fun way to find out how much you *really* know about marriage. Take the following quiz.

THE LOVE DOCTOR'S MARRIAGE IQ QUIZ

For each statement, circle TRUE or FALSE to best describe your belief, then see below for scoring.

1. **TRUE FALSE** Not only do opposites attract, but they are more likely to stay together over the long haul.
2. **TRUE FALSE** Women have more romantic notions and beliefs than men.
3. **TRUE FALSE** A perfect marriage is one with no conflict.
4. **TRUE FALSE** Men and women are equally affected by marital conflict.
5. **TRUE FALSE** If you are truly in love with your spouse, passion will never fade.
6. **TRUE FALSE** Once trust is broken in a marriage, it can never be regained.
7. **TRUE FALSE** Having a child together will strengthen your marriage.
8. **TRUE FALSE** Jealousy is a sign of true love and caring.
9. **TRUE FALSE** Maintaining separate lives is the key to a happy marriage.
10. **TRUE FALSE** To be happy, you need to talk about challenges and problems often.

SCORING: Count up the number of times you circled "False." That number is your Marriage Intelligence Score.

0–3 Your knowledge of the sexes and marriage is based largely on cultural myths found on TV and in movies, handed-down folk wisdom, and perhaps even on your own experiences and those of friends or family. Don't feel bad—you have a lot of company. Read on to learn the realities behind these myths.

4-7 Your marriage IQ is fairly typical. You've probably had some real-life experiences that cleared up a few of these misconceptions. Still, you're not absolutely convinced that some of your beliefs don't have a strong basis in truth. Once you find out what relationship studies reveal, you might change your mind.

8-10 Congratulations! You have a solid knowledge about marriage already, and you're in a great position to learn more. Much of the information in these next few pages will offer you new insights about love and marriage. Read on!

Let's dig down and explore the science-based facts that debunk each of these ten myths, one by one. Remember, each time you break down an assumption or myth-based belief, you are creating more realistic expectations about marriage. By creating realistic expectations, you are avoiding the potential frustration that could later erupt in your marriage. This is what I mean by expect less and get more out of your relationship. It is a key step to taking your marriage from good to really great!

MYTH #1. OPPOSITES ATTRACT AND STAY TOGETHER.

Reality: Similarity plays a key role in relationship longevity and marital happiness.

People are often physically attracted to their opposite. But believe it or not, this attraction is short-term. My own research and that of others shows that *similarities* are what actually keep people together for the long term and lead to the most successful, happy partnerships. There is no danger in having *too much* in common with your spouse, despite what the myth would have you believe. Does this mean you have to like the same music or food? Or share similar hobbies and interests? No, if you like to play golf and she prefers yoga, that's no big deal. If you like chick flicks but he is a foreign documentary aficionado, that's fine. Such differences—as long as they don't dominate the relationship—can spice up a relationship. However, what you do need to have in common are your *key life values.*

In my study, those couples who share similar key life values—such as putting the same importance on religion or agreeing on how children should be taught and cared for—are the happiest couples over time. A couple can share all-important life values even when they are of two different races, religions, or have very dissimilar social backgrounds. Such differences are not as essential for marital happiness as the two partners' similarity in basic life values.

In general, researchers have found that "attitudinal similarity"—or the sharing of beliefs, opinions, likes, and lifestyle—are what really help two people get along. There are three reasons for this. First, similarity validates our own view of the world. In other words, people who hold similar values provide us with support and validation of our own opinions. Second, similarity leads to less conflict and tension between spouses. You and your spouse won't end up disagreeing about those issues that are *most* important to you: your core values and underlying attitudes. And third, similarity often leads to positive mutual feelings. The fact is that we simply like others who share similar viewpoints because we expect they'll like us in return.

When Danielle and Nathan, one of the happy couples in my study, are asked why they are happy in their marriage, one of the most important things they mention is their similarity when it comes to morals or shared underlying values.

> Danielle specifically mentions religion. "Our church is a central focus in our lives. Even though Nate was raised Catholic [earlier she identified herself and her church as Pentecostal], he shares my values. Now we go to church and Bible study together. Pastor D. is a big part of our lives. God is the glue that keeps our marriage bond strong."

If you believe the myth, you may feel that your spouse or marriage is boring. You may get frustrated by his or her predictability, and fantasize about what it would be like to be with someone completely different from you—someone exotic, mysterious, maybe even slightly dangerous.

DID YOU KNOW...

A recent article in the *Journal of Personality and Social Psychology*, by Shanhong Luo and colleagues at the University of Iowa, may explain why Woody Allen types like Annie Halls. If you are neurotic and anxious, you are more likely to be attracted to someone else who is neurotic and anxious than to someone who is rational and calm. They found that sharing quirky personality characteristics plays an important role in marital happiness.

Once you stop believing the myth, you will gain a deeper appreciation for the values you and your spouse share. You will see why your similarities drew you together in the first place—and how they keep you connected and truly happy. You can easily eliminate the frustration you feel by doing something wildly different with your spouse—something out of your normal routine—rather than yearning for a companion who is radically different from you.

MYTH #2. WOMEN ARE MORE ROMANTIC THAN MEN.

Reality: Studies show that men are more romantic in their beliefs than women.

Brace yourself, because here is another relationship myth that surprises most people. Unlike the images of the swooning,

THE LOVE DOCTOR'S CHECKLIST OF COMPATIBILITY FACTORS

Below is a list of ten compatibility factors. If you and your spouse are compatible in four or more of these essential categories, you are likely to be compatible with each other.

- ❏ Willing to try new things that the other likes.
- ❏ Consider each other good friends.
- ❏ Like each other's family.
- ❏ Like each other's friends.
- ❏ Each has personal habits/hygiene the other can live with.
- ❏ Share religious or political beliefs.
- ❏ Are similar in terms of wanting (or not wanting) children and how to raise them.
- ❏ Have similar spending habits/relationship to money.
- ❏ Have intellectual compatibility—easy, fun, or stimulating to talk to.
- ❏ Have physical compatibility—good kisser, good sex, or physically warm.

tongue-tied starlets from the silver screen, research finds that men actually have more romantic attitudes and opinions about love than women do. When researchers talk about *romanticism*, they are referring to a person's general beliefs about love—not one's feelings about a specific person and his or her behaviors.

Two leading relationship researchers, Susan Sprecher and Sandra Metts, were interested in whether romanticism differed between men and women. They asked men and women how much they agreed with statements such as: True love can overcome any obstacle; True love can strike anytime; There is one person who will inspire true love for us. They were surprised to find that men, rather than women, are more likely to believe that love conquers all, that love at first sight really does happen, and that love is necessary before commitment. Men are also more likely than women to think that if you can just love someone enough, nothing else matters. Males tend to believe love should be more passionate than women generally do. These are all romanticized views about love, rather than more rational or pragmatic notions of love.

I was genuinely surprised by the number of men in my study who were smitten with their wives long before their wives even took them seriously. It was a noticeable pattern in many of the narratives. Every couple was asked to describe how they met and what the courtship was like. Their narratives, which included phrases from the husbands like "she didn't know I existed" and "I had to wear her down until she finally gave in" confirm the finding that men, at least in the beginning of relationships, give up their hearts more easily than women. Very often the men resorted to romantic ploys— proposing on one knee with an oversized teddy bear or sending flowers every day—to woo and wow their future wives! I found this to be very interesting.

If you believe the myth, and you are a man, you may feel frustrated by your wife's pragmatic approach to lovemaking and romance. For example, you may be put off by the fact that she

WHO IS MORE ROMANTIC, YOU OR YOUR SPOUSE?

It can be helpful to know how you and your spouse rate on the romanticism scale. If she or he gets a higher score than you do, it can clue you in to your spouse's expectations and beliefs. Circle the answer that most honestly represents your belief, and see below for scoring.

1. True love can strike at any time.
   1—Strongly Disagree 2—Disagree 3—Agree 4—Strongly Agree

2. Only one person will inspire true love for us.
   1—Strongly Disagree 2—Disagree 3—Agree 4—Strongly Agree

3. When it comes to partners, we should follow our feelings, rather than base our choices of partners on more rational considerations.
   1—Strongly Disagree 2—Disagree 3—Agree 4—Strongly Agree

4. True love can overcome any obstacle.
   1—Strongly Disagree 2—Disagree 3—Agree 4—Strongly Agree

5. Passion will last—it won't fade with time.
   1—Strongly Disagree 2—Disagree 3—Agree 4—Strongly Agree

SCORING: Add up your points across the five statements for a total score.

5–9   You are a realist. You are probably more interested in a partner who can get along with your eccentric parents than one who makes passes at you in public.

> **10–15** You may have an active fantasy life, but you are still firmly attached to the idea that a partner should be, above all else, a source of security and your anchor in life.
>
> **16–20** You are a romantic. You can list the best on-screen kisses of all time—because you've watched them over and over! You see the two of you madly in love at ninety and still whispering sweet nothings in each other's ears.

wants to schedule a "date" with you after the kids have gone to bed—as long as it ends before her favorite TV show comes on! If you're a woman, you may feel frustrated by his amorous attention and the way he idealizes you and your relationship.

Once you stop believing the myth, you will gain insight into each other's behavior. In fact, you may discover that both *his* romanticism and *her* practical approach to love have their advantages.

MYTH #3. A PERFECT RELATIONSHIP MEANS NO CONFLICT.

Reality: A lack of conflict means you are not dealing with things that matter.

Many couples believe that if they are fighting, they are doomed. It's simply not true! Although it might sound impressive to say "we never fight," the reality is if you don't

> ### DID YOU KNOW...
>
> Men fall in love faster than women do. When both dating and married couples are asked at what point they first fell in love with their spouse, men report falling in love earlier in the relationship than women do.

disagree with your spouse, you probably aren't talking about important issues or concerns. In a surprising finding from my long-term study on marriage, couples were asked if they have tensions or differences about six topics: money, own family, spouse's family, how to spend leisure time, religious beliefs, and children. Those couples who said "no" to all six topics were also the couples who were *not very happy over time*! Couples could also voluntarily say, "We don't/we never disagree." Again, these were *not* the happy couples. The happy couples in my study readily admit that they fight. But what makes happy marriages different from unhappy ones is that the spouses learn how to deal with conflict in a healthy, productive manner.

This story of my patients Paul and Abigail is a good example of how the "fighting is bad" myth can affect a relationship.

Paul and Abigail have been married for seven years. Paul was extremely worried because he and Abigail seemed to fight all the time lately. And it was always about different topics, in his view: Who's doing more work around the house, why he leaves his socks on the floor, how come he never buys food, and so on. Paul told me he was tired of the nattering, but found himself tongue-tied and stricken with anxiety every time Abigail found a new fault to bring up. Was their relationship in serious trouble, he wanted to know.

Paul has always believed fighting is a precursor to serious problems, because he saw his own parents fight and eventually divorce. He had an unrealistic expectation that happily married couples shouldn't fight. So he clammed up when Abigail would complain, and dread was beginning to take its toll on him. Like Paul, most of us fear conflict—and sometimes try to avoid it completely—because we believe that any amount of conflict with our spouse is negative and can't be good for the health of the relationship. But in reality, it's so important to remember that all marriages have their ups and downs, and that conflict with your spouse is not only perfectly normal, but can lead to new discoveries. For example, when Paul and Abigail talked with me about how they felt about each other, each of them had generally positive views of their partnership. What they needed was to get to the root of their conflict. It turned out that Abigail felt Paul was taking her for granted. Paul, on the other hand, felt criticized and unloved. Once they aired their deeper concerns in a calm and direct way, the domestic details that had seemed so important became relatively easy to fix.

Most studies show that the key to marital happiness is not

the *amount* of conflict you have with your spouse, but the *ratio of positive to negative experiences.* We'll talk more about this critical ratio, which turns out to be something of a formula for marital happiness, in Step 5.

If you believe the myth, you are setting yourself up for frustration. That's because two individuals from different backgrounds, families, and with different habits will inevitably disagree. Expecting no conflict is unrealistic.

Once you stop believing the myth, you will be able to accept that conflict with your spouse is healthy and normal. This will enable you to meet issues head-on without fear. You can see moments of conflict as opportunities to delve more deeply into your spouse's feelings, anxieties, concerns, and needs. That's a great way to ease frustration. In Step 5, we will discuss how to best approach conflict with your spouse.

MYTH #4. MEN AND WOMEN ARE EQUALLY BOTHERED BY CONFLICT.

Reality: Women view marital conflict quite differently than men do, and are more troubled by it than their husbands.

Most of us expect our spouse to think about conflict in the same way we do. Unfortunately, it is not so. If you think your husband is stewing over yesterday's argument and obsessing over what you said in anger before he left for work, think again. When we look at the couples in my study, an unex-

DID YOU KNOW...

If too much housework and child care causes conflict in your dual-earner marriage, maybe you *shouldn't* hire outside help. A study published in *Social Science Quarterly* found that when working spouses got outside help with household chores and caregiving to relieve stress, marital conflicts *increased*. The researchers theorized that when outsiders are hired to take care of the household chores and/or provide caregiving to children or elders, the working couple somehow feels less committed to their marriage and family.

pected finding emerges. We learn that the meaning of conflict is drastically different for husbands and wives. And the big message is this: Recognizing this gender difference turns out to be *very important* in determining whether you can defuse the frustration in your marriage.

Wives in my study who report high conflict with their spouses are significantly less happy in their marriages. For men, high conflict is not predictive of their marital happiness. This is because men and women, in a very fundamental way, deal differently with conflict. Some of this difference is due to social expectations and different learning experiences that encourage women to be more relationship oriented. Women have a tendency to analyze and overanalyze their relationships more than men. Women are more sensitive about conflicts and problems that arise, wish to resolve them at all costs,

> ### CONFLICT TIP
>
> Many couples fall into the trap of discussing difficult topics at night, in the bedroom. That's a big Love Doctor no-no! Never bring your disagreements into the bedroom—you don't want negative feelings associated with the room of love, comfort, and passion.

and don't let them go easily. Men, on the other hand, have a difficult time even remembering what the last conflict was, when it was, and what it was about! When questioned, husbands will usually say the fight was resolved. When women are asked to describe the same conflict, their responses are much different. They remember details. Women will insist the disagreement was *not* resolved, because they feel that more talk is needed to resolve why and when it happened in the first place. Women tend to hold on to that conflict for two to three days. In contrast, men compartmentalize it in their minds. The fight doesn't linger; men are through with it and are already thinking about putting gas into the riding mower after work.

New gender research also shows that men's and women's hormones may shape their emotions and memory. Women remember more details surrounding the conflict—and they remember them for longer periods of time, sometimes years. Scientists also believe that the relatively new finding that women have more fibers connecting the two hemispheres of their brain than men do may explain why, during an argument, a problem for her becomes intricate, with many sources of information interconnected. Men, on the other hand, have brains that help them separate themselves from the problem, and view one issue at a time. In the end, both biological characteristics and social learning experiences may make men and women think and cope differently, and this may explain problems they have when fighting.

Here's an example you can no doubt relate to. A wife comes up to her husband the day after they just had a big fight. She wants to talk about the disagreement again. Why did he say what he did yesterday? And why can't they think of another solution to resolve what they were talking about? "Huh?" the husband responds. "What were we talking about yesterday, and what did I say that upset you?" He's not trying to annoy her. Chances are, he really *doesn't* remember! He has already experienced the conflict and moved on. But she has been thinking about it nonstop for most of the day. Both spouses are truly frustrated with each other and it leads to anger, disappointment, and an even bigger fight than the day before.

If you believe the myth, and you are a man, you will get frustrated because you expect your wife to let the conflict go, just like you. You'll believe that she's obsessing needlessly. You have no desire to revisit who said what. If you are the wife, you will be frustrated because you assume your husband is avoiding the big issues, and you expect him to think, rehash, and analyze the conflict until it's settled to your satisfaction.

DID YOU KNOW...

Helen R. Weingarten and Elizabeth Douvan, both psychologists from University of Michigan, observed that men and women ask different questions when they problem solve. When problem solving, women will ask you *what you mean*. They are focused on the underlying reasons why you did what you did. In contrast, men will ask you *where this is going*. Men's problem solving is very task oriented and focused on the future implications of the discussion.

Once you stop believing the myth, you will have more insight into your spouse's behavior next time a big argument surfaces. If you are the wife, you will try to stop obsessing over the details of the conflict. You'll understand that conflict is inevitable, and sometimes, the little things don't get resolved. If you are the husband, you'll be more understanding of her while she's rehashing the conflict. Knowing the ways in which men and women deal with conflict differently will lead you to try new tactics, appreciate your spouse's perspective, and move on. Again, the best ways to approach conflict with your spouse will be discussed in Step 5.

TIP FOR WOMEN

Find the best situation to bring the topic up (again). Avoid talking when he's tired, hungry, or just coming home. I encourage couples to start dialogue over the phone or email. Tell your spouse what you want to talk about and your feelings about the specific issue. Then, ask if you can make an appointment with him today or tomorrow to discuss the issue and your feelings further. This takes the edge off intense emotions before a face-to-face conversation. It also gives your spouse time to think about his response.

TIP FOR MEN

If you're looking forward to "make-up sex" after an argument, all you have to do is say "I'm really sorry" or "I'll make a real effort to change." A study of gender differences during interpersonal conflict, published in the journal *Sex Roles*, found that women were more angry than men with unresolved disputes, but actually felt *happy* after arguments if they ended with either an apology or a compromise!

MYTH #5. IF YOU ARE TRULY IN LOVE WITH YOUR SPOUSE, PASSION WILL NEVER FADE.

Reality: Passion declines over time but is replaced with a different type of love that is associated with marriage longevity and happiness.

The relationship expectation I get asked about most concerns the topic of passion and excitement in a marriage. People usually expect that "rush of newness" to last longer than it inevitably does. When the excitement declines or even disappears, they begin to worry about their marriage and feel frustrated by the humdrum aspects of their love life.

This is typical for most married couples, according to the leading relationship research studies on the topic. The hot desire, desperate longing, and ever-present passion couples feel at the beginning of their courtship—and even well into the first months and years of their marriage—usually decrease in intensity over time for most couples. The good news is that *love itself* doesn't decrease.

There appear to be two distinct types of love that occur in relationships: a love full of passion—that's the first-blush love when the relationship is young—and a love filled with friendship that keeps relationships together and truly happy over the long term. This second type, called "companionate love," is characterized by friendship, intimacy, and commitment—and has been found to actually *increase* over the course of a relationship. Studies continue to find that relationships lasting fifteen years or more include high levels of companionate love. When I have asked couples married forty to fifty years, "What do you think is the key to your relationship happiness lasting for so long?" virtually all respond with the same answer. They attribute their great bond to the friendship and support of their spouses. Companionate love, in other words, is a key factor in marriage longevity and happiness.

I am reminded of a couple that came to one of my marriage enrichment workshops several years ago, after thirty-five years of marriage. By the end of the weekend, most of the younger participants felt this couple, Clark and Roberta, could have *taught* the seminar. I'll never forget what Clark said of his partnership with Roberta. "She's my best friend, my girlfriend, my wife, my sister. She's my perfect companion. For every roll, you know, there's a frankfurter, and she's mine." We all laughed at this piece of old-fashioned wisdom, but there wasn't a dry eye in the place either.

Among the married couples in my study, romance and passion are definitely not the focus of the happiest couples. I found that those couples who continue to romanticize their relationships over time are actually less happy and less likely to manage stressful challenges in their future together. Happy couples from my study, on the other hand, take a more pragmatic approach to their married lives together. They are less caught up in examining what it means to be a married couple and the romantic components of their marriages. They are more focused on living day to day and managing married life. One happy couple in my marriage study actually likened their partnership to a business. "Together, we run a very profitable operation here," the husband said. "And the benefits aren't bad either!"

But in order for partners to stay healthy and happy, passion, romance, and sexuality are also essential in any long-term marriage, a finding that is illustrated by all of the exceptionally happy couples whom you'll meet in the course of reading this book. Where there's a happy marriage, we've found there is also good sex and plenty of passion. When the passion does start to decline over time—which it will—*take heart*. It can be reignited when both partners make small behavioral changes. All it requires is a mutual desire to try. What most couples find surprising is how easy it is to get the passion going and the sex revved up again—even after a decade or more of marriage. The passion may not distract you all day at work or keep you awake at night like it did when you were first dating, but I think you will find that the feelings are still there and the quality of lovemaking is as good—and often better—than it was in the early years of marriage. In Step 4, you will learn fabulously simple and fun ways to reignite and recharge your love life.

If you believe the myth, you may feel frustrated by the lack of spark in your marriage. This could lead you to think that something is wrong with your relationship, or to start looking elsewhere for sexual gratification and excitement.

Once you stop believing the myth, you will realize it's normal for passion to decrease after the first few years of marriage. Rather than being frustrated and unhappy, you can commit to rebuilding passion in your marriage and finding new ways to boost your love life. It's easy when both spouses desire it.

PASSION TIP

If you're looking for more passion in your marriage, book a night away from home for at least one night—even if it's a hotel room in your town. Research finds that wives feel more amorous when they are in an unfamiliar setting—one without kids and domestic reminders such as undone laundry or dirty dishes.

MYTH #6. ONCE TRUST IS BROKEN IN A MARRIAGE, IT CAN NEVER BE REGAINED.

Reality: Trust can be rebuilt, but it takes work and commitment on both spouses' parts.

Many people believe a major betrayal signals the marriage is over. We know trust is an important and necessary aspect of any relationship—and essential for long-term happiness. In order for a marriage to move forward, you need to develop and nurture a level of trust. When we trust our spouse, we believe that he or she tells us the truth. We also believe that his or her intentions toward us are positive. Studies show that if you trust your spouse, this reduces your inhibitions and worries, and you are free to share feelings and dreams with each other. Once this sharing occurs, you also feel closer and more connected to him or her. Whether you can trust your spouse depends on your ability to trust others, and whether your spouse is trustworthy (i.e., is dependable, reliable, and honest). So in any relationship, trust is always a two-way street; we need to be able to trust others, and we need to find a partner who is trustworthy.

A wife named Nancy talked about a breach of trust early in her marriage to Greg.

They had both just moved out of their parents' houses after they got married. Nancy describes this as a rough time for them financially. The couple was living in a small apartment and working opposite shifts. "Greg would stay out all night—because he worked the lobster shift midnight to eight—and then go out with his friends and drink beer until noon at the diner or at one of his buddies' houses. Can you imagine?" She describes this period as "devastating," because she was trying to get pregnant, never saw her new husband, and recalls that he was either "drunk or hungover," when she did see him. Nancy talks about being suspicious about his activities while she was at work, and about losing trust. She says it took a full year after he quit that job for her to feel as though he was really "in the marriage." During this same period, Greg stopped drinking when Nancy told him "he would have to either choose alcohol or me and our future family."

For Nancy, Greg's drinking and other lifestyle choices felt like a betrayal. When they both became committed to the health of the marriage, everything improved rapidly. This couple has been happy together since 1989.

At the beginning of a relationship, trust takes time to develop. If you are in a new relationship, pay attention, and wait and see whether trust grows and expands as time goes on. Trust follows a clear pattern in most relationships: The more you trust your partner, the more your partner is likely to trust you in return. One of the questions people frequently ask is whether it is easier for women or men to trust their partners. It turns out that there are no differences between men and women in their desire or ability to trust others. We're so used to hearing about the *differences* between men and women that it's nice to find out that there are actually some areas that we have in common!

When your spouse has an affair or betrays your trust in some other way (e.g., gambling or lying), the trust that the two of you have built up over time is broken. In order for your marriage to continue and for you to be happy, you must rebuild the trust. This takes even longer to develop after a betrayal, as the story of Nancy and Greg illustrates.

I get asked all the time about the issue of trust. Whether the husband is bothered by *her* office flirtation or the wife discovers *his* secret credit card, trust issues are very touchy and worrisome subjects for couples. They ask me, "Can I ever regain trust in my spouse, now that it has been broken?" The answer is yes, but it takes conscious effort and commitment from both spouses. From my experience with patients, both partners are often not on the same page about where they see their future together. An affair, which is an extreme betrayal of trust, is an external sign of an internal desire for change on the part of one partner. Most times, an affair can signify that both partners are not willing to do whatever it takes to rebuild the relationship. This is why research reveals that only one out of four couples can move beyond an affair (or other major betrayal) and regain the necessary trust in their relationship. At times, it may feel like finding another relationship would be so much easier. Rebuilding trust takes a long time; this issue will not resolve itself in a few weeks or months. However, my experience with patients has shown me that the longer you stick with it, the more likely you will succeed. Expect occasional setbacks. You need to keep in mind that when your relationship first started, it took a long time for trust to develop. Know that it takes even longer for trust to be rebuilt the second time around.

In addition, after a betrayal it is very common for both men and women to feel anger toward their spouses, even far into the future. You may be able to forgive him or her, but you will never forget what happened. These memories periodically bring back the anger. It is what you do with that anger that is important.

I have some simple but effective tips on how to rebuild trust with your spouse, if he or she has recently betrayed you. I have used these with couples in my practice and seminars many times.

THE LOVE DOCTOR'S SEVEN TIPS FOR REBUILDING TRUST WITH YOUR SPOUSE

1. *Set a specific time period*—six weeks, six months—when you and your spouse will commit to work on the relationship and agree not to give up. During this time period, the

trust-breaker is not allowed to see or communicate with the object of his or her infidelity. You and your partner need to spend time with each other and communicate directly. Start from this point forward and see whether your spouse can display dependable and reliable behavior.

2. *There needs to be a heartfelt apology.* A sincere apology is one where the betrayer takes responsibility for his or her actions. Whether you accept your spouse's apology may depend on whether this is a one-time behavior or whether this is a consistent pattern in your relationship.

3. *Discuss both spouses' perspectives.* Do you have a sense of why your spouse had the affair or betrayed you? Does your spouse understand how you feel and how this affected your relationship? You don't need to agree, but you do need to air and understand each other's feelings, motives, and expectations. Make sure this discussion and understanding goes both ways.

4. *Express anger in a constructive way.* Some amount of anger is beneficial; it motivates you to move forward in your life and marriage. But don't attack your spouse, physically or psychologically. Sometimes writing an angry letter to him or her, then destroying it, helps.

5. *Don't blame yourself for the betrayal.* It is sometimes easy for the person who was betrayed to blame herself or himself. Your self-esteem and self-worth are not defined by or dependent on your spouse's behaviors and actions.

6. *Make a list of the positive things in your relationship.* Right now, it may be difficult to think of the positive qualities in your relationship. It will take time, but coming up with

these qualities, alongside your spouse, is important because you both need to remember and talk about the good that brought the two of you together in the first place. Yes, you might be hurting and in great pain, but if you can think beyond this grief and anger to what was positive in the relationship, this will gradually help you see the light at the end of the tunnel.

7. *Seek assistance from a counselor or therapist.* This situation can be very challenging, regardless of how strong a relationship or an individual might be. It can be tough to break a consistent pattern of hurt and anger. A therapist's perspective and help can be very beneficial, especially in the beginning.

If you believe the myth, whether you are the betrayer or the spouse whose trust was betrayed, then you will likely feel frustrated by the state of your marriage, pessimistic about your future, and powerless to repair it.

Once you stop believing the myth, you can both begin the hard work of rebuilding trust. Rather than feeling frustrated and angry that things didn't turn out the way you had expected, you can rechannel your energy into the future of your marriage.

DID YOU KNOW...

Research by Rebecca Ammon at the University of North Florida shows that men get more upset by *sexual* infidelity, while women get more upset by *emotional* infidelity—as when a man has a crush on a female friend. It also found that the more you value a long-term relationship, the more likely you are to be distressed by emotional infidelity, regardless of your gender.

MYTH #7. HAVING A CHILD TOGETHER WILL STRENGTHEN YOUR MARRIAGE.

Reality: Marital happiness decreases after children are born.

Another very common myth about marriage, especially among newlyweds, is that having a child together will create a stronger bond and increase intimacy between spouses. When childless couples are asked whether one or more children will strengthen a marriage, the majority answer yes (about 69 percent). But real life turns out to be the *opposite*. Although children are wonderful, amazing, enriching, and bring joy to your life, being a parent is stressful and sometimes even overwhelming. Parents don't get enough sleep; they can't focus their attention on the relationship; they bicker about money, child care, and household chores; and they have little time for themselves.

If you and your spouse feel as though marriage with kids is a grind, it may help you to remember that this sentiment is quite typical. Before children, a husband and wife can spend a lot of time together and focus on their relationship. Once a child is born, the couple must now focus their attention and energies on the child. Children inevitably require major changes, compromises, and sacrifices. This is true whether you bring children into a marriage or you have children together.

When we ask participants in my study to name the event that affected them most as a couple, most say it was the birth of their first child. Even among couples who characterized themselves as very happy every year we have interviewed them, it is typical to hear one or both spouses talk about children as disruptive to the marriage, trying, or difficult. Yet these same couples will name children as the best thing that ever happened to them. See what I mean? For most married couples, having children may be a hardship in many respects, but it very often brings couples closer together in the long run.

The happy couples in my marriage study take a holistic view of marriage after children. This means they see the big picture and talk about how every aspect of family life fits together, interconnects, and ultimately *strengthens* or adds character to a marriage. These couples see children as an essential part of their marriages, and dealing with children and family issues becomes essential to their love relationships. The happy couples with children whom we have observed over the years seem to be able to shuffle priorities, so that children, individual spouses, and the marriage relationship itself all take turns at the top of the pile. In contrast, couples who put their relationships on hold while they are raising kids—or put vastly more focus on the kids' needs than on their own—end up in marriages where one or both of the spouses feels distressed.

In terms of the effect of children on happiness, my study has identified a pattern that other marriage researchers have confirmed as well. It is what we call the U-shaped curve. Marital happiness is very high at the beginning of marriage. Couples are in what is known as the "honeymoon aura." Then, after about two to three years, marital happiness declines and continues to decline until about twenty-five years of marriage, when it begins to increase again. And, believe it or not, it isn't until about thirty-five years of marriage that marital happiness is higher than in those first honeymoon aura years! My own research shows that one reason marital happiness declines in those early years of marriage is because of the added pressures and stressors of starting and maintaining a home together—with or without children. The addition of children, however, significantly increases the strain on many new couples.

Now, this decline in happiness doesn't mean the two spouses/parents love each other less. It merely means that the more responsibilities and roles you have (e.g., spouse, parent, employee, boss, student, daughter, volunteer, etc.), the less time and energy you can give to any of them—and the less happy you are in any one role as well. Big message: Don't believe the myth that children strengthen marriages. If you do, once the parenting challenges arise, you will think there is something wrong with you and your marriage. Instead, continue to invest time and energy into your marriage and relationship, and keep focusing on the family as an intricate mosaic that is comprised of you, your spouse, your partnership, and the children.

If you believe the myth, then you and your spouse will be frustrated by how much added stress the kids are putting on the marriage. That frustration could easily turn into resentment, parenting squabbles, and unhappiness.

Once you stop believing the myth, you can see the bigger picture—how to integrate and accommodate different personalities, needs, and styles, and how to co-manage family challenges with your spouse. I see over and over that couples who are able to integrate their role as parent with that of spouse characterize themselves as very happy. In Steps 3 and 4, you will learn some simple strategies for prioritizing your relationship, even after you have children.

MYTH #8. JEALOUSY IS A SIGN OF LOVE AND CARING.

Reality: Jealousy has more to do with insecurity than love.

Jealousy is a common experience in romantic relationships. We feel jealous when we think we are going to lose a relationship we really value. Another common misconception about marriage is that if your spouse becomes possessively jealous, this means he or she really loves you. Or that if your spouse doesn't act jealous, then he or she doesn't really care. But research psychologists know jealousy and possessiveness usually stem from fear and low self-esteem. The experience of feeling jealous says more about your spouse's own issues and insecurities than about the intensity of his or her love for you.

Contrary to popular belief, research shows that men and women do not differ in their tendency toward jealousy. Instead, men and women respond very differently to the *experience* of jealousy. When men experience jealousy, they feel angry and hurt, and are much more likely to retaliate, express anger at their wives, or consider leaving. In contrast, women respond to jealousy by trying to improve or preserve the relationship. They react by wanting to change something in the partnership or in themselves. Both responses can be very damaging to a marriage.

It's also important to realize there are two types of jealousy. *Reactive jealousy* is when you become aware of an actual threat to a relationship you value. The event may not be current or it may be anticipated in the future, but the jealousy is always in response to a realistic danger. *Suspicious jealousy* occurs when your spouse hasn't misbehaved and your suspicions do not fit with, or are not warranted by, the facts at hand. Suspicious jealousy often results in worried and mistrustful behaviors to confirm suspicions. This distinction is important, because most people feel reactive jealousy when they realize their spouse has been unfaithful, but people vary a great deal in their tendencies to feel suspicious jealousy in the absence of any real threat.

If you believe the myth, and you are feeling insecure in your marriage, you may try to make your spouse jealous in order to

DID YOU KNOW...

A study published in *Cognition and Emotion,* by Todd Shackelford, David Buss, and Kevin Bennett, found that men have more difficulty forgiving a sexual infidelity than women do, and are more likely than women to terminate the relationship after they've discovered the betrayal.

"test" his or her love. This is an indirect way to communicate, and will only end in frustration. Conversely, if you find yourself reacting jealously to your spouse's friends, outside activities, or other situations, you may wrongly assume that you are simply behaving as any loving partner would behave. Your spouse, on the other hand, will feel frustrated by your lack of trust.

Once you stop believing the myth, you can avoid a lot of frustration that is eating away at your happiness. Once you know your spouse's jealousy (or your own) has more to do with insecurity, the two of you will have a good starting place to begin a healthy, constructive dialogue. In Step 5, you will learn some simple strategies to help you or your spouse change jealous behaviors that are detrimental to your happiness as a couple.

> ## JEALOUSY TIP
>
> The more your identity is tied to the marriage (e.g., your economic status, social status, self-worth, etc.), the more suspicious jealousy you are likely to feel. If you often feel suspicious jealousy toward your partner, work on boosting your independence and sharpening your definition of yourself outside of being his or her spouse.

MYTH #9. HAVING SEPARATE LIVES KEEPS COUPLES TOGETHER LONG TERM.

Reality: Interdependence is what keeps couples together.

How many times have you heard someone say of his or her spouse, "Oh, we never see each other and live in completely different worlds. That's probably why we're still together!" Not so fast. Studies show if both partners are *interdependent* socially, emotionally, and financially, there is a greater incentive to be together. Interdependence means spouses' lives are intertwined—what one does or has affects the other, and vice versa.

Peter and Joy, a happy couple from my study, are a good example of what interdependence feels like in a marriage.

Peter is a computer engineer and Joy is a massage therapist. He describes their marriage as "hectic but happy."

The couple spends a lot of time with each other's families who live nearby. They have three children, and Joy says of their parenting, "We split the chores pretty well, between chauffeuring the kids, cooking meals, and taking them to doctors' appointments." They both say they have individual interests and enjoy these with other people. Peter is a biker and Joy has no interest in that. Joy is interested in Buddhism, and spends one evening a week at the local monastery. Joy characterizes her family life as a "big pot of soup—we're always throwing new ingredients into the pot, and it just keeps getting better." When Peter is interviewed, he talks about how Joy "lets me be who I am."

On one hand, some *independence* is a good thing. You don't want your spouse to be the sun you revolve around. Moreover, separate interests and friends are good for you and good for the marriage. For example, if you have a burning desire to hike a mountain and your spouse hates vigorous outdoor exercise, then going by yourself or with a friend is fine. Being able to do your own thing is positive and healthy for the relationship. Having new experiences and sharing them with your spouse can also add excitement to your marriage. You will learn much more about this in Step 4.

But on the other hand, too much separateness and independence isn't a good thing for the marriage. Spouses who live totally separate lives quickly forget the joys of being together and begin to wonder why they are even married to each other. In the social arena of life, if one of you has separate friends and interests, it is important to discuss those friends and interests with your spouse. You also want to make sure your friends and interests intermingle once in a while.

To put these findings about interdependence into action, you could: (1) have a party and invite each spouse's friends, (2) make sure you go on a vacation together rather than take separate vacations, or (3) invite your spouse into one of your special interests—he shows you how to play tennis and you show him how to enjoy vegetarian cuisine, for instance.

If you believe the myth, you may turn too often to friends, work, and outside activities as ways to escape some of the real issues facing your marriage. For example, if you feel as though you and your spouse are growing apart, and that this is just par for the course, you will feel increasingly frustrated and unfulfilled in the marriage.

Once you stop believing the myth, you can avoid most of the frustration by talking with and spending more time with your spouse. My study of marriage found that couples who work on acquiring common interests as the years go by are much happier than couples in which one or both spouses gets increasingly involved in activities that exclude their partner. This is because the act of being open to your spouse's interests and making an effort to be involved in activities that bring you together creates interdependence and promotes a sense of intimacy and connectedness.

WHEN ARE SEPARATE LIVES OKAY?

Maintaining separate friends, vacations, and interests in a marriage is fine once in a while, as long as you agree to all three of the following statements:

- I have separate friends and interests, but I also enjoy spending time with my spouse.

- I don't feel as though I need space from my spouse.

- I feel totally comfortable having my spouse spend time with my friends.

MYTH #10. TO BE HAPPY, YOU NEED TO TALK ABOUT CHALLENGES AND PROBLEMS OFTEN.

Reality: Men and women have very different tolerances for how often it is necessary to discuss the relationship, so pick your battles carefully.

In order for intimacy to occur in a marriage, both spouses need to share and disclose private and important matters to each other. Also, direct communication with your spouse is the best way to get your concerns or suspicions heard. It is essential to be able to talk to your husband or wife, because when couples feel as though they can't resolve differences with their spouses, they feel dissatisfied and frustrated.

On the other hand, I have found that couples who arrive at a balance between excessive venting and being circumspect

> **DID YOU KNOW...**
>
> The couples in my study who enjoy the happiest marriages expressed that they did not feel competitive, in terms of getting enough time or attention, with their spouses' friends or family early in their marriages.

enjoy better-quality and longer-lasting marriages. It might surprise you to learn that the happily married couples in my study do not spend a lot of time in conscious relationship maintenance or talk. Over time then, for happy couples, married life begins to flow without too much attention, and the pressure to talk about the relationship diminishes. In Step 3 you will learn more about how happily married couples pick their battles carefully.

One happy husband from my marriage study describes his relationship talk this way, and his attitude is quite typical of other happy couples:

We've learned how to do "check-ins" once in a while— that's when I ask her how she's feeling about stuff, and she asks me the same. These conversations usually last about five minutes. We just don't make a big deal of it. If marriage has to be a constant struggle, then what's the point?

But it turns out that after the first few years of marriage there also are gender differences in the need and rewards for disclosure or conscious relationship talk. Women, as a rule, have a *positive association* with relationship talk. It makes them feel connected, bonded, and happy. Men, however, *do not enjoy* relationship talk, associating it with marital problems, blame, or unhappiness. In Step 3, you will learn more about this gender disparity, as well as extremely simple ways you can both use this knowledge to enhance your happiness as a couple.

When these findings are taken together, it means that wives should pick their battles when it comes to talking about their feelings and the relationship. Remember that while you may see this type of talk as beneficial and rewarding, he sees it as a problem that he caused and now it is something he needs to "fix." For husbands, remember that women build intimacy in their relationships by talking to one another, unlike your male relationships where you bond by "doing" things together. So when she wants to talk about the relationship, this is how she builds intimacy and closeness. It's a fact that women like to talk about the relationship once in a while— even when things are going well and there are no problems. It feels reassuring to them.

If you believe the myth, you may find yourself overanalyzing and picking apart every aspect of your relationship. Whether you are a man or woman, excessive relationship talk will lead to frustration—and will definitely take the fun out of marriage.

Once you stop believing the myth, you will both be relieved to know it's okay to let things slide once in a while, to mentally acknowledge a flaw in his or her thinking without saying it aloud, and to agree to disagree sometimes. If it's no big deal in the grand scheme of things, let it go and you will find you have a lot less frustration—and a lot more harmony and contentment—with your spouse.

PERSONAL EXPECTATIONS OF YOUR SPOUSE AND MARRIAGE

Now that you know some of your relationship beliefs are not supported by scientific research, you can begin to address your own *personal* expectations for your spouse and your marriage. We all have expectations for our spouse (how he or she should behave or treat us) and for our marriage (how it should be now and how it should develop in the future). Just as frustration can develop when our general expectations of relationships are unrealistic, so too can frustration arise when we aren't clear and we don't communicate our personal expectations to our spouse—and when our spouse doesn't communicate his or her personal expectations to us.

The following exercises will help you and your spouse dig deeply into your own wants and needs so you can identify and articulate your expectations to each other. *If your spouse doesn't know what is in your head and heart, he or she won't be able to understand why you are frustrated.* I have designed these easy but powerful exercises as a way to reduce the resentment that can eat away the happiness and joy from your marriage.

I have identified the sixteen most common marriage expectations. The beauty of science, in my mind, is that it gives us raw material to then transform into useful tips and tools we can put into practice right away.

I developed the Marriage Expectations Toolkit (see below) so couples could use it to improve their relationships. It provides a quick way to find out what you currently expect from your spouse, and what he or she expects from you. Simply put, I have found that one of the qualities all happy couples share is they have a clear understanding of each other's expectations. I have shared it throughout the years with people in couples therapy and workshops, and the results are stunning and immediate. Achieving happiness in your marriage does not have to be complicated or time-consuming. But it helps to have some tools.

THE MARRIAGE EXPECTATIONS TOOLKIT

Here are the sixteen most common marriage expectations as reported by the married couples in my long-term study, followed by exercises to do individually and with your spouse.

1. You should cool off before you say too much if you're fighting.
2. You should enjoy leisure time together.
3. You should control the way you express anger with each other.
4. You should each have an equal say about all important matters.

5. You should feel that your spouse would never hurt or deceive you.

6. You should be ready and willing to compromise when you disagree.

7. You should have some private time away from each other.

8. You should be allowed to keep some of your money separate.

9. You should always say what is on your mind.

10. You should always settle a fight quickly.

11. You should try not to be critical of your spouse.

12. You should share equally in household chores.

13. You should know the people your spouse spends leisure time with.

14. You should listen carefully to each other's point of view.

15. You should take time for your own individual friends.

16. You should take the time to understand each other's sexual needs.

Exercise #1: On a piece of paper, you and your spouse should individually rank the importance of each statement to your own marriage, on a scale of 1 to 4, where:

1 = Very important to my marriage

2 = Fairly important to my marriage

3 = Not very important to my marriage

4 = Not important at all to my marriage

Exercise #2: From your top-ranked expectations (usually ranked 1s and 2s), each of you circle your top-two expectations from the list of sixteen. These are the ones that are absolutely the most important to you right now. (Your answers will tend to change over time when this exercise is repeated.)

Exercise #3: Put a star next to the two expectations you predict your spouse will rank as his or her top two. Then, exchange answers.

Now for the fun part! Could you identify your spouse's top-two expectations from the list? Did your spouse correctly predict yours? Differences in expectations between you and your spouse are fine. Appreciate and celebrate your differences. The most important part of this exercise is that your husband or wife discovers what you expect, and how much it means to you. You can revisit this exercise every year and get totally different outcomes. I have found that when couples are aware of each other's expectations—and their relative importance is brought out into the open—they experience less frustration and more marital happiness. Each partner now knows what the other thinks should happen in the marriage and neither gets frustrated as frequently or as intensely.

This simple exercise is one of the easiest ways I have seen for couples to get more out of their relationship by defusing the frustration that sabotages marital happiness. Consider the story of Joanne and Michael, one of the happy couples in my study.

When Joanne and Michael ranked their personal expectations as described above, they each said that the most important marriage expectation for them was trust: "You should feel that your spouse would never hurt or deceive you." The second most important marriage expectation for both of them describes an effective way to manage conflict: "You should be ready and willing to compromise when you disagree." Both were quick to say they weren't at all surprised to read the other's top expectations and ratings for each of the sixteen personal marriage expectations, and they weren't even surprised that their top two were identical. They mentioned that they were careful to talk to each other a lot and get a sense of what each other wanted and desired out of their marriage.

DID YOU KNOW...

The marriage expectation that was named "most important" by the happiest couples in my study was: "You should feel that your spouse would never hurt or deceive you" (ranked first by 92 percent of men and 96 percent of women). The second most important marriage rule for these happy couples was: "You should listen carefully to each other's point of view." The least important rule for them? "You should be allowed to keep some of your money separate." In general, the men and women in my study were very similar in what personal expectations were important to their marriages.

STEP 1 TAKE-AWAYS

Expect less, get more. This means that the fewer unrealistic expectations you have of your marriage and spouse, the more happiness both of you will experience. This is the first step toward taking your marriage from good to great. Here's a review of what we covered in this chapter:

- The biggest reason marriages fail is frustration.
- Frustration is caused by having unrealistic expectations of your spouse and your marriage.
- By transforming unrealistic expectations into realistic ones, you will avoid the frustration that sabotages marital happiness.
- Unrealistic expectations are usually based on myths.
- To debunk or dispel these myths, it's important to understand the scientific findings that contradict them and provide a basis for new perceptions and behaviors.
- Looking at love, men, women, and relationships through this new, more realistic lens will help you feel more content with your marriage and your spouse.
- The happiest couples are those with the most realistic expectations of their spouses and their relationships.
- Identifying your own personal marriage expectations and sharing these with your spouse is an important step toward making your marriage better.
- Findings show that happy couples are fully aware of what each spouse expects out of the marriage.

2
GIVE INCENTIVES AND REWARDS

Do and say simple things
to keep your partner happy.

When you make your husband or wife feel valued, loved, and supported with simple acts and behaviors, the two of you can move beyond a so-so marriage to one that is exceptional, robust, and enduring. Now that you have learned how to have realistic expectations of your marriage and your spouse, the second step to achieving a truly great marriage is to do and say simple things to keep your partner happy. A happy spouse has plenty of energy for, and interest in, the relationship. A happy spouse is also motivated to make the marriage better and stronger.

When I say these are simple gestures, I really mean it. But the effect on your spouse and on your marriage will be profound. Here's why. Research shows there are three basic needs all people in relationships have: (1) the need for reassurance of self-worth, (2) the need for intimacy and closeness, and (3) the need for assistance. The happiest couples from my study have these three needs met by their spouses. When your spouse makes you feel important, well cared for, and supported, it is easy to reciprocate, and you feel happy to be in that relationship. The best part is, it takes very little to meet these three essential needs.

I will show you how to meet all three needs for your spouse through everyday gestures, acts, and words. The only catch is that men and women typically have different ways their needs get met and different ways they meet their spouses' needs. It is essential to understand these important gender differences—but once you do, the rest is a snap.

AFFECTIVE AFFIRMATION—WHO NEEDS IT MOST?

Learning how to give "affective affirmation" will help you fulfill your spouse's first two needs: the need for reassurance and the need for intimacy. In relationship psychology, affective affirmation consists of words, gestures, or acts that show your spouse that he or she is noticed, appreciated, respected, loved, or desired. Business managers know that employees perform best when they receive frequent positive feedback. The same holds true for your love partner. When I observe happy couples in my study and therapy practice, they all share one trait: They give each other affective affirmation on a regular basis.

One of my most significant and unexpected findings centers on who needs this love and positive feedback the most, husbands or wives. Do you have a guess? The findings show that husbands (more than wives) lack and crave these simple acts of loving-kindness and attention.

Let's look at the reasons why, and then I'll show you simple, practical, well-researched ways to show and express affective affirmation to your spouse.

For the married couples in my study, receiving enough affective affirmation was a critical factor in how happy both husbands and wives said they were in their marriages. However, affective affirmation was *far more important* for husbands than it was for wives. If we view affective affirmation as an indication of how a loved one feels, it makes sense it would be important to marital happiness. But why does it play a more significant role in the husbands' happiness?

When social scientists study women and men, they observe that women, as a rule, get lots of this good stuff—affective affirmation—every day. They get frequent compliments, support, smiles, encouragement, and subtle rewards from family, friends of both genders, coworkers, and even strangers. This kind of talk is ingrained in our culture. "I like your shoes! Pretty smile! Nice to see you! You're an angel!" and so on. If you are a woman, it's probably easy to remember the last time you walked down the street or entered the grocery store and someone declared, "You look great" or "Love your outfit!" This happens all the time to women, so much so that we often take it for granted. The net effect, though, is that women feel affirmed, noticed, admired, and liked almost on a daily basis.

This affective affirmation from the world buoys us up and adds to our sense of self-worth. Women still need affective affirmation from their husbands, of course, but they don't need as much from their husbands in order to feel happy as their husbands need from them. If you think of affective affirmation as an essential vitamin, women usually get plenty of it outside of the love relationship. Men, on the other hand, suffer from a vitamin deficiency; they need much more affective affirmation at home.

If you are a man, can you remember the last time a friend, colleague, or stranger took notice of you and made you feel special with a compliment or some unsolicited positive feedback? Men simply don't get these perks as much as women do, and they are downright starved for them. As mentioned before, the need for reassurance is an *essential basic need* all people in relationships have. It is not trivial. Therefore, a husband's major source of feeling affirmed on a regular basis comes from, guess who? His spouse.

One of my most significant findings is this: When affective affirmation is lacking in the marriage, or when it breaks down, husbands become devastated and distressed and are less happy in their marriages. In contrast, when husbands feel affirmed, noticed, and admired by their wives on a daily basis, they are happy and more fulfilled in their marriages. When we analyzed the data from my study, we found that the presence of affective affirmation was *strongly predictive* of husbands' marital happiness. This important finding has enormous implications for both wives and husbands.

One of the happy couples from my marriage study went

through a rough spot early in their marriage that was exacerbated, in part, by the husband's yearning for everyday affirmation and attention from his wife.

Soon after they got married, Tom and Eliza had their first son. Tom describes this period as a time when Eliza spent more time with their son than with him, and he felt "invisible." During this same period, Tom grew very close to a woman at work, and this close relationship became a huge challenge in the marriage. He would go to bars after work with his work friends, including this woman, and not come home until late. Tom and Eliza admit that they nearly got divorced because of this "almost affair." When Tom discusses this event, he mentions not feeling valued, loved, and supported by Eliza in the first years of his marriage. He says he was "starving for attention and validation from other women."

This story illustrates that when men lack the validation they get from feeling noticed by their wives (affective affirmation), they literally experience it as a hunger and feel distressed. In Tom's case, he sought comfort from a female friend—which could have been disastrous for the marriage had it continued.

When I first learned about the pivotal role affective affirmation plays in husbands' marital happiness a few years ago, I was stunned. I racked my brain trying to remember the last time I gave my *own* husband affective affirmation. I called him at work right away. Without delay, I exclaimed:

THE LOVE DOCTOR'S AFFIRMATION QUIZ

How much do you feel affirmed in your marriage? How much do you affirm your spouse? Take this quiz to find out. These are the same questions we asked the 373 couples in my long-term marriage study. Rate each statement on a scale of 1 to 4, where: 1 = never, 2 = rarely, 3 = sometimes, and 4 = often. See below for scoring.

In the past month how often did you feel that your partner . . .

- made you feel good about having your own ideas and ways of doing things?

- made your life especially interesting and exciting?

- made you feel good about the kind of person you are?

- was especially caring toward you?

SCORING: Add up your points across the four questions for a total score.

4-6 Your partner may love you to pieces, but he or she sure isn't letting you know, through words and actions, that you matter. If you're feeling ignored or taken for granted, read on to find out how you can help your spouse do this for you.

7-9 This score indicates that your partner notices you and gives you some attention, but you are not getting as much affirmation as you desire. Why is this important? Because lacking enough affirmation can lead to feeling neglected and dissatisfied in your marriage. The good news is it's easy to reverse.

10–13 Outsiders probably watch the two of you and admire your relationship. That's because your spouse has no problem outwardly demonstrating that he or she values you. You've got a good marriage. Now it's time to take it to the next level: greatness.

14–16 Congratulations! You've got one fantastic marriage, judging by the amount of attention your spouse pays to making you feel wonderful about yourself. You probably thank your lucky stars every day to have this bond. Keep at it, and above all, reciprocate!

VARIATION: Now think about how affirmed your spouse feels in your marriage. Are you making him or her feel valued and loved on a regular basis? To find out, ask your spouse to take this quiz.

"Sweetie—you are such a worthwhile person. I love you! Your ideas are really important to me, and you make my life exciting and interesting!" There was a slight pause on the other end, and then he said, "Gosh, thanks. Are you okay?"

We chuckle about this now, but it opened my eyes to the fact that up to this point, relationship researchers, including myself, did not fully understand how significant affective affirmation was to husbands' marital happiness. The truth was, I hadn't been giving as much affective affirmation to my own husband as I was getting—from him and from others as well.

Doing and saying simple things to affirm my husband has definitely improved our marriage. I notice, for example, that he literally lights up when I tell him that I admire him, or that those jeans really "show off his body." But it's not just flattery he is responding to. Marriage researchers know that when people receive affective affirmation, it symbolizes a deeper caring and attention. After one of these exchanges, I notice my

DID YOU KNOW...

When the happy couples in my study were asked the questions in the Affirmation Quiz, their answers differed *significantly* from those of other couples—confirming that affirmation plays a crucial role in marital happiness. Consider:

- 43 percent of the happy couples said their spouses "often" made them feel good about having their own ideas and ways of doing things (compared to 27 percent of the other couples).
- 47 percent of the happy couples said their spouses "often" made their life especially interesting and exciting (compared to 22 percent of the other couples).
- 61 percent of the happy couples said their spouses "often" made them feel good about the kind of person they are (compared to 27 percent of the other couples).
- 74 percent of the happy couples said their spouses "often" were especially caring toward them (compared to 46 percent of the other couples).

husband gets into a chipper mood, or seems enormously grateful. Who knew it could take so little?

Gender Differences vis-à-vis Intimacy

We've talked about gender differences related to affective affirmation, but there are also differences in how men and women experience intimacy. Men don't experience closeness and intimacy with outsiders at the same level of intensity as they do with their wives. When relationship researchers talk about intimacy, we don't mean sexual intimacy. Rather, through the scientific lens, intimacy is a feeling of intense connection or a close bond. Men simply don't get as much of this essential attention from their outside relationships because there are differences in how men and women "do" their same-sex friendships or promote closeness in their relationships with others. Some of this is due to innate differences between men and women, but in general, men and women "do" their friendships differently because of variations in socialization or what we teach children to want out of their friendships. And this difference in the nature of friendships starts very early in life.

Young boys engage in rough-and-tumble play with friends (e.g., wrestling or football) and spend more time in larger friendship groups. In contrast, when girls are young, they spend more time one-on-one with friends. Their play is less physical and more about personal interaction, such as playing with dolls and playing house. Even their sports activities are less likely to be contact sports (e.g., hopscotch or tetherball). These types of play and the close, intimate nature of the friendships girls form allow them to cooperate rather than compete. They give affirmation to their playmates more frequently and more comfortably, which creates a sense of closeness. Boys, on the other hand, don't have the same opportunities in their friendships to give and receive affective affirmation. Their style of play is more physical, more competitive, and less emotional.

These differences follow the two genders into adulthood. As adults, women spend more of their same-sex friendship time simply talking, sharing, and giving positive feedback to each other. Men spend more of their time *doing* things. When men get together with their same-sex friends, they engage in activities—not conversations—such as going to a sports event, playing basketball or poker, or watching TV.

You can see how the difference in how men and women experience friendships plays out by imagining a couple having a problem in their relationship. The wife is likely to call her girlfriends to talk, seek advice, and analyze what has happened. The women may spend hours, if not days, deliberating about the situation over the phone or in person. This talking time is therapeutic, rewarding, and affirming to women. But if the husband calls a male friend to get some advice, the men are more likely to shoot some pool or have a drink together. You just can't imagine a male friend responding, "Let's have a cup of tea and explore your feelings."

Thus, same-sex friendships can be bonding for men, but they don't create the necessary intimacy and closeness we all need as human beings. There is evidence that mixed-sex friendships can provide needed closeness and intimacy for men, but even these friendships don't usually provide the kind of everyday affirmation men crave. So when men get married, they are drawn to their wives for the affirmation and closeness they need and desire.

There is also an important difference in the *number* of close friendships or relationships men and women describe, regardless of how they define closeness. Compared to her husband, a woman will usually say she has many more close friendships and family ties (e.g., mother, girlfriends, sisters, coworkers, and especially children, who are strong sources of feeling loved as an adult). In contrast, men usually admit to having only a handful of friends or people they feel close to—and often it is only their wives whom they describe feeling really connected with.

To illustrate this gender difference, I usually have my patients participate in the Circle Diagram Exercise. This exercise helps couples identify the people in their lives they are closest to, and how their close bonds and relationships may be different from their spouses'. It gets them thinking about the quality of emotional connections they maintain with others. I ask each member of the couple to do the exercise separately, and then share the information with his or her partner. The results are fascinating. The circles of the husbands and wives are *completely* different, and this helps couples—especially women—understand the relative importance of their role in the marriage.

To do this exercise, draw five concentric circles, like a target. List the five people you feel closest to. Put yourself ("me") in the middle circle—the bull's-eye—and then, using the first names of each person, place each name in the circle that best represents how close you feel to that individual. The closer that person is to the middle, the closer you feel emotionally to him or her.

Men typically put their wives right next to them in the inner circle. The other four people are usually placed in the outer circles of the diagram. While husbands come up with five close relationships, only the marital relationship gets a premier spot in the inner circle.

Women's circle diagrams radically differ from their husbands'. Women typically have no problem listing their five closest relationships, and often ask me if they can list seven or eight. After their husbands, children, siblings, and parents, they have a tough time deciding which friends to include or exclude. But even more amazing is that all five closest relationships—including their marriages—are typically smack dab in the inner circle. And if not in the innermost circle, a close relationship is in the next circle nearest to the center. When a woman decides she feels close to someone, that person becomes part of her inner circle.

PUTTING THIS KNOWLEDGE TO WORK WITH YOUR SPOUSE

How can this knowledge about the differences between what the two genders need help you? For a man, you can now clearly see the critical role your wife plays in your own validation and self-esteem. Have you put her in a central, singularly empowered role by not forging close friendships with others? Once you are able to acknowledge the nature and importance of her role in fulfilling your need for validation and intimacy,

CIRCLE DIAGRAM EXERCISE

TYPICAL WIFE (MARY)

Tim, Amy,
me, John,
kids, sister,
Mom & Dad,
Sue, Shel

TYPICAL HUSBAND (JOHN)

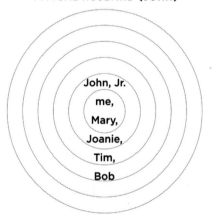

John, Jr.

me,

Mary,

Joanie,

Tim,

Bob

you have two options. First, you can accept it and not fight it. You can say, okay, I'm just going to know that my wife is the person in my life who will give me a sense of value and closeness. By doing this, you are simply admitting that, given our culture and what is acceptable for men to do and feel, you perhaps haven't had the means or taken the opportunity to make other really intimate friendships. Your second option is to accept and understand the role that your wife plays in your happiness and also to make an effort to build friendships with others that are strong and validating. This may mean joining a men's group, a prayer study group, a book club, or a tennis or golf foursome so that you can have more contact with men, and create opportunities for others to get to know you outside of work, on a personal basis.

For women, the knowledge that you are the main provider of reassurance and intimacy for your husband gives you incredible power. A woman is often amazed to discover that by saying and doing small, simple things, she can make an enormous difference in how her husband feels in the marriage—and in turn, how he responds to her. Most women have no idea that they have this much ability to influence their husbands' long-term happiness and short-term behavior. I, myself, was even surprised at the effect it had in my own marriage.

HOW TO GIVE AFFECTIVE AFFIRMATION

There are two ways to give rewards and positive affirmation to fulfill your spouse's needs for reassurance and intimacy. The first way is by *saying* and second is by *doing*. It turns out, not surprisingly, that men and women express affective affirmation differently—and often respond to different styles of affective affirmation. In my study, women typically reassured husbands verbally, while men typically gave their wives affective affirmation through actions.

Here are two very sweet stories two wives told about their husbands:

> J'NAI: My husband always fills my car with gas when I need it, especially during the winter months. He doesn't want me to stand in the cold while I get gas. Also, early in the morning, he goes out to scrape the ice and snow off my windshield and windows.
>
> PEARL: After losing six precious babies to miscarriages and having recovered from four operations, we cherish each other with small expressions. Once, when we were getting dressed up for a formal occasion, I had buckles on my shoes and my husband (without me asking) got down on his knees and gently buckled my shoes for me. The sparkle in his eyes told me he is still as much in love with me as I am with him.

Each wife recognized that these small acts of kindness were her husband's way of letting her know she's valued.

One reason understanding gender differences like these is important is because it can lead to valuable insights that really help you in your own marriage. For example, look at what your spouse says and does. Are you "missing" what he or she is trying to tell you?

A wife may complain to her girlfriends that her husband never says he loves her. Meanwhile, he may be showing his love and appreciation for her regularly—but she doesn't put two and two together and see that his researching their next vacation or inflating her tires is man-speak for "You matter to me." Alternately, men are more action oriented. A husband may complain that his wife never comes to watch his Sunday softball games. His wife, however, ends every phone call with "Love ya." So essentially, he wasn't really hearing her words. And she wasn't seeing that he wanted to be *shown* affirmation, not *told*.

Once you understand that men and women have different ways of expressing affective affirmation, it will really open your eyes. Both spouses in a good marriage usually have an "aha" moment when they realize their partners have been telling them all along—in ways large and small—that they are valued and loved. The problem was simply that the expression of love got lost in translation.

Armando and June are one of the happy couples in my study. I think that this little story Armando tells about his wife during one of his individual interviews really nails how it feels when you recognize that your spouse is showing you affective affirmation.

It's hard to explain what June does. It's not like she tells me day in and day out that she loves me. But she really lets me know in different ways that I'm her "man." You know, like when she goes to the grocery store, she comes back with the spicy sauce only I like on my steak. She calls

> ## SELF-ESTEEM TIP
>
> To boost your wife's self-esteem, tell her she's beautiful. To bolster your husband's self-esteem, tell him he's hot. In a study by psychologist Todd Shackelford, wives were more likely to have high self-esteem when their husbands complimented their looks. Husbands didn't care about their own looks—but they *did* care about their desirability. The self-esteem of husbands studied fell sharply when their wives didn't compliment their sexiness.

me when I work late at the restaurant. She makes me feel like I'm the only man there is—I don't know, like I'm making a hundred grand instead of just forty.

A second reason to pay attention to the two styles of giving affective affirmation is so you can find new ways to reassure your spouse. If he's not responding to "I love you," try giving him a neck massage instead. If she's not responding to the fact that you fixed that squeaky cabinet hinge that was driving her crazy, try telling her how happy you are to see her at the end of your long workday.

It's really not very hard to show your spouse through small endearments that he or she matters to you. Frequent, reciprocal affective affirmation is one of the predictors of a really great marriage. The results from my study show that couples who gave frequent, reciprocal affective affirmation were

---

TIP FOR MEN

You don't need to buy expensive jewelry for your wife to show her she's loved. Instead, just tell her: "If I had it to do all over, I'd marry you again in a heartbeat."

---

almost *twice as likely* to describe themselves as happy in their marriage.

Keep in mind that verbal affirmation can be articulated over the phone, in email, or in person. There is no etiquette or formal rule that an endearment has to be delivered face-to-face. Sometimes a surprise phone call in the middle of the day delivers even more bang than a kiss when you get home. The point is to show affective affirmation often—and in all kinds of ways.

Here's how one patient put my findings on affective affirmation into action:

Thirty-five-year-old Marcelle was starting to feel like her ten-year marriage had hit a rut. She loved Sam, but things just didn't seem that wonderful anymore. She decided to try some new behaviors. She randomly kissed Sam before dinner one night. She surprised him by starting the coffee in the morning—usually his job—so it would be ready when he came downstairs for breakfast. She complimented him on his new haircut another day. She told him

DID YOU KNOW...

A study funded by the National Science Foundation showed that spouses who feel chronically less valued in the relationship are more negative, rejecting, and critical of their spouses than those who feel secure about their partner's regard for them. Spouses who feel highly valued by their partners, on the other hand, tend to reframe marital conflicts or their partner's bad moods in a positive light.

she liked his smart take on a movie they'd seen. Sounds small, right? Marcelle reported that Sam seemed instantly happier and was more attentive to her after these small changes. Marcelle in turn felt more bonded to Sam than she had felt in years. In fact, everything felt different at home. Marcelle had no idea that such small—and, she thought, trivial—actions would make such a difference.

Marcelle's small acts of affective affirmation had a big result because she was showing Sam she valued him (the first need in relationships) and felt intimately connected to him (the second need). She used a combination of words and actions to reassure Sam that he was important to her and that she loved him. So instead of doing something *you* would like, ask yourself, "How can I show my spouse I notice him and he matters?" Marcelle gave her husband a kiss and had coffee ready for him in the morning. No words need to accompany these acts of affirmation. To him, they spoke volumes. Could it be that easy to keep your partner happy? Indeed, it really is that simple!

WORDS: WHAT TO SAY TO KEEP YOUR SPOUSE HAPPY

There are countless ways to tell your spouse you care about him or her: You're handsome. You're sexy. You're my favorite cook. You're a great kisser. You're so much fun. You're a riot. You're the best dad/mom.

There's no need for an expensive gift next Valentine's Day or anniversary. Instead, go to the store and buy a card. Write one of the phrases below on your card. Or just say them aloud. These are simple statements that will make your spouse feel loved, cared for, noticed, and valued.

1. I love you even more now than when we were first married. (This tells your spouse you are still interested, and gives him or her a sense of hopefulness, reassurance, and security.)
2. You are my best friend/the best lover/the best husband or wife. (This says that you notice who your spouse really is and do not take him or her for granted.)
3. I would still choose you. (Every partner needs to hear these words on occasion. They are affirming, nurturing, and appreciative. It is also a reminder that you are renewing your commitment to this relationship.)
4. Let's plan _____ [a vacation, a date, getting pregnant]. (This says you want your spouse in your future, and he or she is your top priority.)

5. I've really noticed that you have _____ [been helping more around the house, been working really hard these past several weeks, been helping your mother through rough times, etc.]. (This shows you are paying attention to the particulars of your spouse's life, and that he or she matters.)

ACTS: BEST THINGS TO DO FOR YOUR SPOUSE

The key to *showing* affective affirmation is to see the world through your spouse's eyes. What does your husband or wife love or need? Think about your partner's habits or some specific challenges he or she faces.

Is your wife always running out of cash? Slip some bills in her purse as a surprise. Is she always rushing around? Offer to take the kids to sports practice for a change. Is he stressed out at work? Make his favorite dinner tonight. Is he too busy to fix the garage door? Have it fixed by a handyman without telling him. Take a walk after dinner. Buy tickets to the theater. Kiss and hug your partner. Whisper something romantic. Lock eyes with him or her for longer than usual, and flash a smile or wink. Compliment him or her. Spontaneously grab his or her hand when you are walking somewhere. Buy your spouse a small gift—a book, a CD, flowers, chocolate, slippers, or gloves.

The key here is to make small gestures that show you're paying attention. That's all it takes to make your spouse feel as though he or she is valued and loved. My research shows that when couples give affective affirmation and fulfill the first two needs for each other—the need for reassurance and the need for intimacy—they are likely to be very happy together.

HOW TO MEET THE THIRD NEED: THE NEED FOR ASSISTANCE

The need for assistance is the third need people have in relationships. Everyone needs help and support at some time. The happy couples in my study expressed that their partner was "there when they needed them." This feeling of being able to count on your spouse is a key to marital happiness.

Here's a touching story one wife from a happy couple told about her husband:

> I recently had surgery that required two nights and three days in the hospital, and not once did he leave my side. He even slept in a vinyl fold-down chair for two nights and didn't complain once. Even with all the poems he's written and thoughtful things he's done, sleeping in that chair that wasn't meant to be slept in was the most romantic thing he's ever done.

In a marriage, situations will occur in which one partner requires some type of support from the other partner—whether it's a small thing, like coming to get you when your car breaks down, or a big one, such as comforting you after a tragedy.

We typically think support is needed at times that are particularly stressful, such as an illness, an accident, or the loss of

DID YOU KNOW...

If your spouse wants help getting healthy—and you want to support him or her—the best way to help is to be a good role model. According to the National Institute on Aging, when one spouse quits smoking or drinking, has a cholesterol screening, or gets a flu shot, the other spouse is more likely to follow suit.

a job. But it would be a mistake to overlook the everyday kind of social support that involves your spouse listening to you when you need to talk, cheering you up when you are feeling down, or doing chores when you are exhausted from work or other family responsibilities.

In fact, one of the common themes in virtually every single happy couple's story is the presence of mutual support and assistance. The happy couples in my study all mentioned that they can count on their spouses for support and assistance, no matter what the issue, and regardless of whether the issue is big or small. Listen to this account.

Wayne is a middle manager at a large insurance company, and Lakeisha is an administrator at a social services organization. They live very comfortably, and in their first year of marriage were able to buy a three-bedroom house together. Lakeisha and Wayne both say there was a bit of an adjustment period in the early years of their marriage, especially when Lakeisha went back to school to get her master's degree and had their first child.

Wayne was very supportive emotionally of Lakeisha's decision to go back to school after they got married. They discussed it ahead of time, and he knew it would make her happy and that it would also help her get a promotion and a higher salary at work. Wayne says that he took care of a lot of the housework when she went back to school and after their daughter was born. Most surprising to Wayne was how happy that made Lakeisha feel, so he still does a lot around the house. For Lakeisha, Wayne's help around the house was essential for her. Without it, she has no idea how she could have handled everything. She says of Wayne, "I couldn't have gotten as far in my career without Wayne."

For Wayne, the feeling is mutual. He shares one story about how his twin sister and only remaining family member was in a serious car accident. Wayne was at an insurance conference in the next state and couldn't get home in time. Lakeisha sent their daughter to a friend's house, and spent the next eighteen hours by Wayne's sister's side, holding her hand. The sister did eventually recover, and Wayne attributes this to his wife. He remembers this event as one of the most powerful examples of his wife's support, expressing the feeling that his wife was able to be his surrogate, or to emotionally and physically replace him, at a time when he was unable to be present. "If my sister had died, part of me would have died with her. Lake knew that."

Lakeisha and Wayne talk a lot about support for each other. They say the best thing about being married is having someone there to support and assist you—for both big and small things in life.

TWO KINDS OF SUPPORT

Relationship research shows that men typically like to give what we call "instrumental support" to their partners—the kind of help characterized by advice and solutions to a problem. Men like to "fix" or "solve" the problem so that it goes away. So if your wife is telling you about a difficult time with a client and you respond by asking her to make a list of the positive and negative things she likes about work, or tell her how to negotiate a better contract, you are giving her instrumental support.

Interestingly, this type of support is not always effective for women, because research shows that women typically prefer to receive "emotional support"—the kind of help characterized by empathetic or comforting feedback. A woman wants to feel as if her husband is on her side, but she does not necessarily want to take action right away. So the next time your wife is complaining, for instance, about a heated dispute with a relative, and you want to show your support, try just listening to her, and then console her, or tell her how difficult this problem must be for her, or simply let her know you can really hear and relate to what she's feeling.

In contrast, when men are having a bad day at work, research indicates that the most effective way a wife can support him is to give him advice and try to solve the problem with him. Instrumental support is not the same as solving the problem *for* him. It means he wants concrete feedback and validation during his own problem-solving process. As the wife, you might listen to his laments and then say, "Are you going to bring this up with your boss? How do you think he'll approach it?"

Always bear in mind that the type of support you give to your partner must match the type of support your partner *wants* to receive; otherwise, it is not supportive or very helpful. Men and women, at different times, may crave either type of support—instrumental or emotional. I always tell my patients and workshop participants that the next time your spouse is in need of support, ask him or her, "Are you looking for some practical advice, or would you prefer that I just listen?" Asking your spouse which type of support he or she wants is an act of real sensitivity and caring.

Here is another place where my marriage research has helped me in my own relationship. As a therapist, I am trained to listen to people's problems and let them know, by mirroring back to them what they've said, that I am listening and that I understand. Often the mere act of feeling "heard" helps therapy patients come to their own solution. But when my husband was having a particularly difficult problem with his elderly father's health care and I slipped into my therapist's role, he wasn't a happy camper. He didn't want emotional support. In fact, he came right out and said, "I know you *sympathize*. But that's not really helping me figure this thing out right now." He couldn't have been clearer; what he wanted and needed from me was *instrumental support.* I snapped into action and asked him outright: "What can I do for you? Would you like my advice, or can I make a couple of phone calls and help you sort through the insurance paperwork?" I've learned that by asking him what kind of help he needs, I can be a better source of support.

One of the key factors leading to a successful marriage is the quality and consistency of support two people provide for each other. A relationship built upon mutual support will overcome just about any obstacle two individuals encounter along the way. Support can be something as small as being sympathetic when our partner has had a stressful day, or as complex and involved as providing expertise, time, and energy when a partner is embarking on a new business endeavor. Support can take many forms. In the broadest sense, it is the willingness of two people in a relationship to lift each other up and encourage each other to be the best they can be. Support is also the willingness of the individuals to be there for each other through both good times and bad.

What's important here is that in a great marriage, spouses ask each other for support, and expect to *be* asked. Many of us, however, are afraid to ask our spouse for support when we really need it. We think it is a sign of personal weakness. We should be able to fix or solve things on our own. Also, we don't want to be a "burden" on our loved ones. Bear in mind, though, that everyone needs support from his or her partner at some time. My research shows that the more willing you and your partner are to support each other and be supported, the stronger your marital bond will become. In fact, over 90

THE LOVE DOCTOR'S FIVE TIPS FOR
ASKING FOR SUPPORT

Sometimes, it can be difficult to ask your spouse for help and support. Here are tips for doing it:

1. **Identify the need.** Examine the problem at hand and what you really need from your spouse. Do you need a shoulder to cry on and a sympathetic ear? Do you need concrete advice and practical solutions? Do you need validation that your decision or solution is sound? Do you just need to vent and get it all out of your system?

2. **Communicate the need.** Talk to your spouse about the problem and what you specifically need. Don't expect your spouse to read your mind.

3. **Appreciate and validate the help.** Remember that people have different styles of helping: Some are serious, some use humor, some jump right in, some hold back awhile. Appreciate all the help your spouse is able to offer.

4. **Coaching is okay.** If your spouse isn't helping you—or is, in fact, being critical or counterproductive—it's all right to give him or her some coaching. Try saying, "Honey, this isn't that helpful. But here's what *would* be helpful."

5. **Continue to seek help.** When things are going well, make sure you continue to seek support from your spouse—not just during the really stressful times. Remember that taking and giving support on a regular basis is important for your mental health, and for the relationship as well.

> ### DID YOU KNOW...
>
> Relative levels of the hormone testosterone in couples could play a critical role in how much social support wives give to their husbands. This interesting finding by researchers at Penn State found that wives in the study provided more social support to their husbands when the wife had higher testosterone levels (relative to other women) and her husband had lower testosterone (relative to other men).

percent of the happy couples in my study felt that their spouse was someone they could count on *often* to support them. These couples voluntarily reported that having a supportive spouse was a significant part of why they felt very happy in their marriages.

STEP 2 TAKE-AWAYS

To keep your spouse happy, give frequent incentives and rewards. Saying and doing small, simple things yields big results, and is one of the easiest ways to take your marriage from good to great. Here's a review of what we covered in this chapter:

- People have three things they need from a love relationship: the need to feel valued (reassurance), the need for connection (intimacy), and the need for assistance (support).

- Affective affirmation—the act of showing through a gesture, words, or act that you notice, appreciate, value, and care for your spouse—accomplishes the first two needs.

- There are two ways of giving affective affirmation—by *saying* and by *doing*. In general, women respond more to verbal affirmation, while men respond more to actions that demonstrate affirmation.

- The happiest married couples in my study were those that gave each other frequent affective affirmation.

- Feeling affirmed is important to marital happiness, but more so for husbands than for wives. Husbands who do not receive enough affective affirmation from their wives often become distressed and unhappy in their marriages.

- Men are starved for affective affirmation from their wives, because they get less of it from the outside world. Women tend to need less affective affirmation from their husbands, because they get more of it from the outside world.

- Women have enormous power to change the quality of their marriages by giving their husbands more affective affirmation.

- By understanding gender differences in how we need and perceive affective affirmation, wives and husbands can give and receive it better. In doing so consciously and frequently, they will feel more valued by and closer to their spouses.

- In successful marriages, wives and husbands both feel their spouses are supportive. Women are more comfortable giving, and often prefer getting, *emotional support.* Men are more comfortable giving, and often prefer getting, *instrumental support*—concrete suggestions and advice intended to "fix" a problem.
- My research shows that the more couples give support to and get support from their spouses, the happier they are in their marriages.

3
HAVE DAILY BRIEFINGS

Practice the Ten-Minute Rule
to really get to know your spouse.

You have now learned that developing realistic expectations of your relationship and keeping your spouse happy with frequent affirmation and support are two critical steps to enrich your marriage and make it stronger and happier. The third important step along the road to a truly great marriage is to really get to know your spouse.

One trait shared by happy couples in my marriage study is that they are intimately familiar with each other's inner lives and social worlds. In addition to knowing their spouse's daily routine and personal preferences, they also know what makes each other tick. They know what is important to their spouses, how the other person feels, and what the other person thinks and dreams about. In short, they have an *intimate* knowledge of each other. My study shows that marital happiness is contingent, in part, on how deeply and intimately the two partners know each other. In fact, a whopping 98 percent of the happy spouses in my study say they "intimately know and understand" their partners.

So how do you get to know your spouse really well? It only takes ten minutes a day, and I'm going to show you why this seemingly small activity of holding daily briefings, which I call the "Ten-Minute Rule," is so important, and how to do it. Couples differ in what they talk about with each other, but I found that the frequent exchange of intimate knowledge between spouses is a major predictor of marital happiness. Importantly, my data show that over 50 percent of the happy spouses, when asked how frequently they revealed very intimate things about themselves or their feelings to their spouses, reported they do this "often," as opposed to only 19 percent of the nonhappy couples who gave this answer. (The other answers they could choose were "sometimes," "rarely," or "never.") Given these findings, the Ten-Minute Rule may turn out to be the most significant thing that ever happened to your marriage.

You will learn practical strategies, tips, and tricks for getting the most out of your daily briefings and other conversations with your spouse. Finally, we will look at several dynamics that often stand in the way of great communication with your spouse—and how you can navigate around them.

THE TEN-MINUTE RULE

What is the Ten-Minute Rule? Put simply, it is a ten-minute daily briefing in which you and your spouse make time to talk about anything under the sun—*except* kids, work, and household tasks or responsibilities. Make no mistake: *Daily briefing talk is not the same as relationship talk*. While it is perfectly okay to use your ten minutes to talk about the relationship every once in a while, the purpose of the daily briefing is not to discuss your marriage; it is to get to know your spouse better. Relationship talk, as you learned in Step 1 and will learn more about at the end of this section, comes with both perils and perks—and should be practiced in moderation.

Get to know your spouse by talking for ten minutes a day? Many people are incredulous when they hear this advice. When I tell couples in my marriage enrichment workshops about the Ten-Minute Rule, there's always someone who says, "Ten minutes? That's a long time!" Or others who say, "Ten minutes? That doesn't seem like long enough!" Then there are those who protest they already know their spouses extremely well. But believe it or not, few couples really take the time to learn about each other, and few couples practice the simple act of daily conversation. From the mere fact of living together, couples know such details as their partners' schedules, taste in food and music, pet peeves, and hygiene habits. However, there is a lot more to find out about your partner, and making the effort to do so will bring you closer and create more happiness in your marriage.

Regardless of which camp you fall into, I guarantee sur-

> ### DID YOU KNOW...
>
> Your iPhone may bring you and your spouse closer. So says a new Pew Research Center study, which found that the Internet and cellphones are creating a "new connectedness" in marriages. Tech-savvy spouses with busy lives keep in touch all day long, and then share news and information at the end of their day.

prises—fun and pleasant ones—when you commit to practicing the Ten-Minute Rule every day. Try it for a week and I think you will be hooked.

WHY THE TEN-MINUTE RULE IS IMPORTANT

Getting to know your spouse better has a number of marital benefits. Learning new information about your partner is exciting. It makes the relationship feel fresh, which in psychological terms is quite important. That freshness and newness you experience mimics the emotional and physical state you were in during the first few years of your marriage, what relationship researchers call the "honeymoon period." That's when passion, interest, and excitement are highest. Yes, I'm saying that the Ten-Minute Rule can help spark passion, but we will talk more about *that* kind of excitement in Step 4. Getting to know your partner better also gives you tools and insights that help you mediate conflict and avoid hurtful situations.

Over time in a marriage, many couples unfortunately mistake their handling of daily tasks and frequent exchanges of practical information for real communication. Just between family, home, and work, there are lots of practical details to manage. You call your spouse, and the two of you discuss who will go grocery shopping, what to make for dinner, and which one of you will pick up your daughter from the newspaper club at school. Then later, at home, the two of you work out tomorrow's schedule, sign a card for your mother-in-law, and help the kids with homework. With scenarios like this, a husband and wife are speaking to each other regularly. But this is not high-quality communication. Instead, these are conversations that focus on daily tasks and maintaining a household. They don't help you learn more about each other.

Daily briefing communication involves exchanges about your personal thoughts, opinions, feelings, goals, and desires. This ten-minute conversation could range from politics to religion, childhood memories to philosophy, current events to TV shows. It's also about hopes for the future, disappointments from the past, accomplishments you are proud of, and fears.

The Ten-Minute Rule will make you and your spouse happier together. I absolutely, positively guarantee it. I get a kick out of what one of my female patients said.

At first when Lloyd and I started practicing the Ten-Minute Rule, we just did it like an exercise—like homework. But in a few days, we both learned something we had never known about the other. We definitely weren't

DID YOU KNOW...

Are you physically separated from your spouse? Are face-to-face exchanges not possible? If your spouse is deployed overseas, frequent email might be a better mode of staying in touch than either phone or videophone. Research by Lieutenant Colonel Simon Pincus and colleagues found that email and snail mail tended to produce less anxiety and a sense of more connectedness on the part of the at-home spouse than "live" communication. They theorized it was because emotions such as hurt, fear, anger, loss, and jealousy are hard to disguise on the phone, and the deployed spouse is then unable to comfort or support the distressed spouse long-distance, leading to estrangement.

expecting to enjoy it so much. When I went on an overseas business trip recently, he emailed me to say that his days just weren't the same without our ten-minute gabfests.

The Ten-Minute Rule is a foolproof way to improve things at home and open up new avenues for relationship exploration. This little activity is almost miraculous—you feel closer, you uncover truths and warning signs, you appreciate each other more, you learn to listen, and you inevitably grow fonder of each other. In relationship psychology, we call this the "mere exposure effect." The mere exposure effect says that when two people are exposed to each other regularly—and especially when they converse—familiarity increases, which in turn leads to liking. You and your spouse, by having daily briefings every day for ten minutes, will become more familiar with each other's inner worlds, which strengthens the bond of happiness between you.

Although they don't call it the Ten-Minute Rule, most of the happy spouses from my long-term study mentioned some variation on regular talking and friendship as important to their happiness over the years. Here is a typical example:

> Ariela, a nurse's aide, and Nathan, an auto worker, report that they talk with each other frequently. Nathan says, "Ari says I'm the only guy this side of the Mississippi who likes to talk more than a woman." They enjoy each other, and speak about how they share everyday experiences and always know what's going on in the other's life. Nathan says his wife is the most interesting person he knows. Ariela remarks that another benefit of being in a partnership is that "you have your best friend right there in marriage." Nathan nods in agreement.

Four Important Areas to Know about Your Partner

You will discover all kinds of things about your spouse simply by making the time to talk every day. I have found there are four vital areas happy couples need to know about each other: friends, stressors, life dreams, and values. By gaining information about each of these areas, spouses become familiar with each other's emotional and social worlds and can take their marriage beyond a so-so marriage to one that is exceptional. So ask yourself the following questions in four areas of your spouse's life, to see if you really know your partner. If you come up blank in one of these four areas, that's a good topic to begin with in your daily briefings.

Friends

Can you name your spouse's best friends? It is important that you know the people your spouse is spending time with and talking to on a regular basis. What are your spouse's closest relationships outside of family? Why? Go ahead and ask these questions. Is there someone at work who makes this list? Is there an old college friend far away who nevertheless feels like a close friend to your spouse? Is that surprising to you? If you know this information about your partner, it means you know him or her pretty well and have been paying attention to his or her activities and inner life. Are you surprised to learn about the people who are on his or her "short list"? Best friends can reveal a lot about your spouse's own personality and character. Bear in mind that the important thing here is that you know *who* your spouse is spending time with. This doesn't mean that you need to *like* these people or even hang out with them.

Stressors

Do you know what stressors your spouse is currently facing? It's really essential that you are attentive to and aware of what your spouse is currently going through. In the last chapter, you learned that feeling supported is one of the basic needs in a relationship. Here, I want you to really find out what keeps your spouse awake at night, what he or she frets about, and who or what is stressing him or her. We all experience different obstacles or challenges that create tension or anxiety in our lives. These challenges, small or large, create personal strain and concern. Stressors could stem from work, family, health, friends, or money challenges. Perhaps we don't like the people we work with or our boss doesn't respect or listen to our creative suggestions. Or maybe our mother or father continues to criticize and comment negatively about how we are raising our children. When you are familiar with your spouse's present challenges, you know what is troubling him or her and you are better able to cope with conflict, anger, or other stress-related behaviors when they arise. Also, you are better able to give your spouse support or assistance when it's needed. Spouses in my study who felt as though they "weren't alone" in dealing with stressful challenges were the happiest.

Life Dreams

Do you know your spouse's life dreams? Do you know what your partner hopes to accomplish in the future? To have a really great marriage, spouses need to talk about their life goals and dreams. I can remember a couple in one of my workshops after they started to do the Ten-Minute Rule. The woman was surprised to find out that her buttoned-up husband, a forty-something high-powered attorney, wished he could take a sabbatical, buy a boat, and sail around the Caribbean for a year. Talking about goals and the future with your mate doesn't necessarily mean these plans will come to fruition. But sharing them has so many benefits, among them: learning about your spouse's level of current discontent or secret yearnings; finding out where your spouse places him- or herself right now in the arc of his or her life; discovering how similar or compatible your future goals are; and showing your spouse the profound interest you can have in his or her life dreams and hopes. This level of discourse will enhance and enrich your marriage in untold ways.

Values

Do you know your spouse's basic values? Generally, most people know their spouse's values. But there are always areas that will surprise you. Do you know which candidate he voted for? Does she believe in financially supporting kids in their twenties? Does he believe there's life after death? Does she think it's okay to serve teens beer or wine at home? Our underlying values and opinions are how we each define ourselves. Not only are values lots of fun to discuss and explore, but finding out how your partner feels about important life issues could have an enormous impact on how the two of you make decisions now and in the future. Asking about value-related topics says to your spouse, "I really want to know you better and I'm paying attention to who you are."

A few years ago, when I first started teaching the Ten-Minute Rule, I talked my husband into trying it with me. We

WELCOME TO YOUR DINNER TOPICS

Do you ever go out to eat with your spouse and the two of you sit in silence? Dinner is a great time to practice the Ten-Minute Rule. Take your time, enjoy, and get to know each other again. Here are some tried-and-true topics:

- What was an important turning point in your life? Why?

- Do you think you are/were closer to your mom or dad? Why?

- What is the one thing you want to be remembered for?

- What is one thing you really want to accomplish in the next two years?

- What is your favorite movie? Why?

- If you could be reincarnated as an animal, what would it be?

- If you were able to work in any other job for a year, what would it be?

- What is really romantic to you?

- What are you most afraid of?

- What age do you feel like inside? Why?

- What do you think are the top-three worst songs of all time?

- What was the one thing you hated most as a kid?

do chat a lot every day because family dinners are a requirement in our household. But this would be different, I told him, because we couldn't count our discussions about work, the kids, or our weekend to-do list as part of our daily ten minutes. Lo and behold, after the very first time we tried it, we learned something astounding about each other's view on whether we wanted doctors to take heroic measures to keep us alive in the event of a traumatic brain injury. I'm not kidding! I can't even remember how we got on the topic, but it turns out he doesn't want anyone to "pull the plug" under any circumstances, and I feel the opposite. That ten-minute conversation led us to write living wills.

THREE WAYS TO ASK GREAT QUESTIONS

There's an art and a science to asking great questions. Masterful interviewers make it look easy. But if you and your spouse have been focusing on the kids, work, or even the bills, it might be a challenge all of a sudden to ask your spouse about topics or things that really matter to him or her. Bear in mind that as long as you are genuinely interested in what he or she has to say, opening up an interesting dialogue with your spouse isn't that difficult.

Before we even get to the questions themselves, though, remember that you are not a psychic when it comes to your spouse. Do not assume you can understand or predict your spouse's thoughts, feelings, and desires without asking. I don't care how long you have known each other or been married— you can't assume. People change. People develop. People forget. What may have been true yesterday or last year may not be true or relevant today. Every time couples in my workshops do the Ten-Minute Rule, longtime spouses inevitably claim that they have learned something brand-new about each other. If they hadn't asked the question, they probably would have assumed (often wrongly) they knew the answer.

Here are three simple and practical tips for asking great questions.

First, Ask Open Questions That Require Thought—Not Just One-Word Answers

These are usually "interrogative-led" questions, beginning with what and why. Too often we ask our partners closed questions. We ask, "How was your day?" or "Did you have a good time?" These questions can be answered with a single word: good, fine, exhausting, yes or no. What we're looking for is disclosure, sharing, details, and depth. So instead, ask open-ended questions that encourage conversation. The following are examples of "what and why" questions for your spouse that require some exposition:

> *"What happened at work today that was exciting or interesting?"*
> *"What did you think about last night's movie?"*
> *"What do you expect from your friendships?"*
> *"What do you like about having kids or not having kids?"*
> *"Why is this job important to you?"*
> *"What do you like/dislike about your commute?"*
> *"Why do you like living in this region/town/neighborhood?"*

Second, Ask Questions That Focus on Specific People or Events Important to Your Spouse

Talk to your partner and encourage conversation directed at activities he or she likes to talk about (even if it isn't your favorite area of discussion). The following are examples of good specific questions that may be important to your spouse:

"Why do you think the Cowboys will win the Super Bowl this weekend?"

"What do you get out of reading Wine Spectator*?"*

"What's it like working with your brother?"

"What do you think our daughter will be like when she's our age?"

"Who do you hope is at the party tonight, and why?"

"Why is the zoning board giving your business such a hard time?"

Third, Ask Questions On a More Personal Level

It's surprising how rarely some couples talk about personal topics. Remember, though, that it was the personal, intimate aspects of your spouse that made you two fall in love to begin with. And guess what? Intimacy through conversation is also what helps keep spouses together. So ask questions that would elicit information your partner wouldn't normally share with others. The more private the information he or she shares, the more you will get to know what your partner is really all about. Here are some examples of good personal questions to ask your spouse:

"Within the last year, what were you most proud of?"

"What is the best thing you remember from your childhood?"

"If you could travel anywhere in the world, where would you like to visit and why?"

"Do you have any regrets in life? What are they?"

"If you could change anything in your current life without suffering any negative consequences, what would it be?"

"Why do you think you and your sister don't get along?"

I'll never forget one couple who came to one of my marriage enrichment workshops and experienced the power of asking good personal questions.

James and Toni were both professors whose only child had recently gone off to college. For the first time in eighteen years they were alone and finding that they felt estranged from each other, so they decided as a couple to explore new avenues of communication. James was very reserved and readily admitted that coming to the workshop was more Toni's idea. But when I instructed the couples, in breakout sessions, to ask questions and practice listening to their spouses, a whole new side of James came out. The first question he asked Toni was about her early sexual experiences. Said Toni afterwards, "I guess it was the inquiring scientist in him coming out, but I don't think we've ever talked that frankly! It made me blush!"

This story illustrates, once again, that we are all complex people, and there are so many things we don't know about our spouses. In a fulfilling marriage, partners are always in a process of discovering new and unexpected things about each other.

THE LOVE DOCTOR'S FIVE TIPS
TO BEING A BETTER LISTENER

1. **Paraphrase what you hear.** Repeat what your partner said back to him or her in your own words. Give your partner a chance to agree that what you heard is what he or she actually meant.

2. **Check out their feelings.** Ask your partner for clarification about what he or she is feeling. Sometimes anger is really frustration, regret is really sadness. Emotions can be misinterpreted. Ask your partner for specifics.

3. **Make what they're saying a priority.** Stay away from distractions while you're listening. You can do this by not answering your phone, not retrieving texts, shutting off the computer, and turning off the TV. Despite what you may think, you cannot do two things at once well.

4. **Validate and respect your partner's point of view.** You don't have to agree with your partner's opinion, but it is important that you allow your partner his or her own feelings.

5. **Listen with your entire body.** The way to show your partner you are listening to what he or she is saying is to show it with your body. Make eye contact, nod your head, turn your body toward your partner, and lean forward rather than away from your partner.

ACTIVE LISTENING

In addition to believing they already know their spouses well enough, many people also feel they are already great listeners. That's probably because someone has told them they are empathetic or helpful. But being empathetic is not the same as being a good listener. When you engage in your daily briefings, I want you to practice what I call *active listening*. Active listening is a conscious behavior that requires more than your ears. It uses your eyes, your body, and your mind. You need to be able to really hear what your partner is saying to you before you ask additional questions. Sometimes we are thinking so hard about what we will ask our partner next, or thinking about a response, that we forget to listen to what he or she is saying. So instead, ask the question, then just relax your body and really try to listen without interrupting aloud or even inside your own head. Make eye contact. When your spouse reaches a stopping place, think for a few seconds, and then respond. If you don't entirely understand, or want more details or clarification, ask for it. You also need to make sure the follow-up questions you ask directly focus on your spouse's answer.

THE PERKS AND PERILS OF RELATIONSHIP TALK

As I mentioned earlier, there is a difference between *relationship talk* and *daily briefing talk*. When I tell couples about the Ten-Minute Rule, it's not uncommon to hear the men groan. That's because they often believe I'm asking them to spend ten minutes a day talking about their relationships. Nothing could be further from the truth!

The happiest couples in my study do not spend a lot of time talking about their relationships. Relationship talk, it turns out, can have some downsides as well as some benefits,

> ## TIP FOR HUSBANDS
>
> Invest in her heart, not in the stock market. A study by University of Virginia sociologists Bradford Wilcox and Steven Nock found that wives ranked their husbands' level of emotional engagement as *more important* to their marital happiness than how much money they made.

as far as marital happiness goes. Let's look at some of the reasons why.

One of the most stunning findings from my study was that, after the first few years of marriage, there are real gender differences in the need for conscious relationship talk and the rewards each gender gets from it. When husbands disclose and communicate their feelings and thoughts about issues in the marriage, this *strongly reinforces* what wives desire in their marriage. Women are more relationship oriented and they like to talk about the relationship—the positives and the negatives. My research found that the more time wives spend with their husbands and disclose personal feelings, talk about their relationships, and tell their spouses what they need, the happier wives are in their marriages.

In contrast, when women disclose their feelings and want to talk about the relationship often, this has *negative* implications for husbands' marital happiness. From the husbands' viewpoint, relationship talk is often interpreted as nagging, and the conversation is seen as problem focused. Husbands are also very likely to think that whatever relationship issue they are discussing is their fault. Perhaps this is because many women aren't knowledgeable about how to bring up a relationship topic in a non-accusatory manner. For example, men are likely to hear blame when women say, "You never share your feelings with me," when what their wives are often trying to express is something more like, "I am feeling lonely in our relationship. How can I make it more comfortable for you to disclose your feelings?" Also, many men, because of what they see, hear, and learn from others, immediately switch into their problem-focused "fix it" mode when they hear "Can we talk about the relationship?"

A man will engage in relationship talk at the beginning of a relationship because he feels it is necessary to get to know his partner, but after the first few years of marriage, this talk has negative implications. My findings show that the more time husbands report they engage in relationship talk with their wives, the *less* happy they are in their marriages.

PUTTING THESE FINDINGS TO WORK

Here is how you can use these findings to make your own marriage happier. For women, it is important to remember that your husband sees relationship talk as if you are bringing up a problem he needs to fix or solve. So don't forget that if you want to discuss your relationship, try to bring up the topic in a nonthreatening manner. Make an effort to start out with a positive statement about what he is doing right, and *then* talk about the relationship. For example, I always tell my husband how much I appreciate his help around the house and with the kids first, before I ask him if we can talk about how we might improve our discussions surrounding money. When you start with a positive statement, and then move on to the relationship, he is less likely to see the relationship talk as problem oriented.

Here's how one wife in a happy couple from my study learned about the dangers of too much relationship talk.

When Sean and I first got together, I was really insecure—I guess because I was really young, and he was ten years older and had a college degree. I used to ask him all the time whether he loved me, how he felt about us, where he saw our marriage in five years, if we could talk about such and such, and stuff like that. One day he just turned to me and said, "Baby, if you keep making problems where none exist, you're gonna have one." I never forgot that. It wasn't that Sean was being mean, it was more like he was saying I was working too hard and overanalyzing everything. And you know what? He was right. Our marriage is really easy and we don't really have to talk about it very often. I just never thought that could be okay.

If you're the husband, you need to keep in mind that women like to talk about the relationship even when things are going well and there are no problems. When they bring

THE LOVE DOCTOR'S RELATIONSHIP-TALK EXERCISE

Try this short exercise that's based on the same questions I asked couples in my long-term study of marriage. The goal is to find out how often you "do" relationship talk with your spouse. Rate each question on a scale of 1 to 4, where: 1 = never, 2 = rarely, 3 = sometimes, and 4 = often.

- How often do you reveal very intimate things about yourself or your personal feelings?

- How often do you talk about the quality of the relationship (e.g., how good it is, how satisfying it is, or how to improve it)?

- How often do you tell your partner what you want or need from the relationship?

- How often do you spend time discussing and trying to work out problems between the two of you?

Now, add up your points across the four questions for a total score. The higher your score, the more frequently you and your spouse talk about the relationship.

If you are a man and your score is 9 or less, keep in mind that relationship talk acts like an aphrodisiac for women. Wives equate intimate talk with intimate feelings. As an experiment, try increasing how often you talk about your marriage this week and see how she responds. You might be pleasantly surprised!

If you are a woman and your score is 10 or above, keep in mind that husbands often equate frequent relationship talk with trouble in the marriage, and that can decrease their sense of happiness. If you love the feeling of intimacy when you discuss your relationship, try talking about something one of you is very passionate about. Often, it's the *intensity* of the conversation—not the topic—that will give you that same feeling of satisfaction and connection with him.

up the relationship or what is happening in the relationship, it doesn't mean they want it fixed or that you are doing something wrong. They just like to rehash events and emotions in the marriage. This kind of talk makes them feel closer to you. And, believe it or not, my research shows that the more women talk about the relationship with you, the more amorous and sexual they feel! Just try to think about it this way: *Relationship talk is like an aphrodisiac for women.* It builds intimacy and closeness for women, and without it, they may feel distant from you and slightly withdrawn from the relationship.

HOW MEN AND WOMEN TALK ABOUT RELATIONSHIPS

Research also shows that men and women talk about relationships in distinct ways. This was first described by the linguist Deborah Tannen, who showed that men do what she calls "report talk," or communicating information about objects, activities, and actions, while women do "rapport talk," which is all about feelings and relationships.

When we interviewed couples in my study, this distinction was evident. For example, notice the difference in how Claire and Stuart responded when we asked them, "How have things changed since your wedding? How are things now?"

> CLAIRE: Things now are pretty good. I think we're starting to get used to each other. We still have some disagreements, but not too many. Oh, we haven't really fought or argued in a long time.
>
> STUART: Busy. I would say things are very busy now. Because she is finishing school. To me, that was a very important thing.

Notice that Claire talks about emotions, how little they are arguing, and the relationship between them. Stuart talks about the schedule and Claire's activities. What does this difference mean? It indicates that, in general, women are more relationship oriented than men. They are more likely to think about their relationship and emotional connections on a daily basis than their husbands are. When you are aware of this key difference between how men and women engage in relationship talk, wives will understand that their husbands are not dodging the important issues, and husbands won't worry that something is wrong in the marriage. Knowing about gender differences in relationship talk helps you understand your partner better.

OBSTACLES TO GREAT COMMUNICATION WITH YOUR SPOUSE

Now let's look at two areas that stand in the way of great communication with your spouse so you can be alert to them and navigate around them.

Miscommunication

The first obstacle to watch out for is miscommunication, which happens when the message we intend to send our partners is not the same message they receive.

Miscommunication typically arises for two reasons. First, miscommunication can occur when there is a discrepancy between what we say (our words) and our behaviors (like our facial expression or our body language). Interestingly, studies show that when a discrepancy like this does occur, the truth usually lies in our behaviors rather than our words. For example, let's say you have been working at home all day by yourself (and enjoying it). Your spouse comes home unexpectedly. You greet your spouse with the verbal message, "Hi, honey. You're home early! How was your day?" At the same time, however, you don't move from your computer, you don't smile or touch your spouse, and your gaze flickers back to the "email-waiting" icon on your screen. Your words may say you're happy to see your spouse, but your body language and behaviors are sending a different message. They are saying: "I'm really busy right now. Why are you here?"

So when your spouse talks to you, be sure to pay attention

DID YOU KNOW...

If you're a newlywed couple, you can improve your chances of marital happiness by eating together once a day. University of Missouri researcher David Schramm found that the biggest challenge newlyweds face is togetherness time. Couples who found everyday ways to spend time together—such as having breakfast or dinner together—were happier and more likely to stay together.

to his or her unspoken messages. If you feel confused, just know that it's probably not all in your mind. Instead, ask questions. Ask your spouse what's up, and really listen to his or her answers. Also bear in mind that your body language can reveal wonders to your spouse about what you really feel or think.

Second, miscommunication can also occur when we misinterpret the message or information our spouse sends to us. Here is a classic example that I use during my marriage enrichment seminars. A husband is sitting on the couch, and he turns to his wife and says: "Let's go out for dinner tonight." This statement can be interpreted in several ways by his wife. Does he mean, "Let's get out of the house, just the two of us, and go somewhere special," which is a positive comment? Or does he mean, "I'm tired of your cooking and I want something else to eat," which has a negative connotation? The message the husband intends to send may not be the same message the wife receives. Instead of assuming you know the hidden meaning behind your spouse's message and risk misreading what is really important to him or her, ask questions! Ask your spouse a specific question in order to clarify what he or she is trying to convey.

Personal Baggage

A second obstacle that can stand in the way of great marital communication is personal baggage. Like it or not, you brought your personal baggage with you into the relationship. Your baggage contains issues you have been dealing with since long before you met your current partner. These might include wounds from complicated family relationships; relationship patterns with ex-lovers; and deep feelings such as rage, fear, or grief from past traumas.

Everyone brings personal baggage into the relationship, but it doesn't have to have a long-term negative impact on your marriage. It is what you do with that emotional baggage that counts. Some of us build walls to protect ourselves from the pain and hurt others might inflict on us. It is safer to keep things to ourselves than risk rejection, invalidation, criticism, or ridicule. These people then carry extra emotional baggage that can get in the way of moving forward by really getting to know their partners and discussing or dealing with what is important to both spouses. It can be hard to unpack and discard old baggage, but I promise you that doing so will lead to a happier marriage.

How can personal baggage affect communication? Let's

> ### DID YOU KNOW...
>
> There is great debate in the scientific literature about whether children of divorce are more likely to repeat the cycle of divorce in their own marriages. In other words, is their emotional baggage from childhood likely to lead to their own divorce? In my study, 36 percent of the black spouses and 24 percent of the white spouses came from families where parents were divorced. My findings are noteworthy: Spouses who had divorced parents were *no more likely* to get divorced or be unhappy than spouses with parents who stayed married. These findings were true for both black and white spouses.

say you have had some pretty unhealthy and unhappy love relationships in your past. If you got used to your former girlfriend losing her cool and threatening to leave every time you brought up certain topics, such as wanting to go camping with your old college roommates, you may hold on to old fears about bringing that topic up with your wife today. So you stuff that topic down into your baggage and there it stays— while you feel resentful, restless, and maybe even angry.

Meanwhile, your wife tells you she's joining a cooking class that will meet every Wednesday night—one that includes four weekend "cuisine tours" a year. You react with anger when she tells you, because you're thinking, "Why does *she* get to travel with her friends while I'm stuck here?" She's surprised at your anger, and can't understand why you're behaving this way. Neither of you is aware that your anger has little to do with the wife's cooking class, but is a carryover from a former hurtful relationship. The solution? Unpack that bag! Don't expect the revelations to come quickly, but the first step to unpacking your personal baggage is to recognize that your current issues or emotions stem from the past rather than your current relationship. Then, use several of your daily briefings to talk about an old pattern you've brought into the marriage—one you'd like to break. Your spouse will appreciate your disclosure, and you will have shrunk one of the barriers that is standing in the way of great communication.

My research shows that in order to take your marriage from good to really great, you need to let go of the past baggage and move on. Unpacking baggage is one of the best ways to let your spouse get to know you better. The personal, profound conversations that unfold when we talk about our baggage are ones that will bring you closer and make communicating easier and more clear in the future. Think of marriage as a single-engine plane that's soaring through life. If you try to come onto that plane with lots of heavy carry-on baggage, you will have to check most of it at the gate, and re-board with one or two smaller, more compact pieces of baggage. That's basically what you need to do in a happy marriage.

STEP 3 TAKE-AWAYS

An essential key to taking your marriage from good to really great is to get to know each other better. The Ten-Minute

THE LOVE DOCTOR'S FIVE TIPS
FOR UNPACKING OLD BAGGAGE

1. **Get rid of the reminders.** Physical things—photos, old furniture, gifts—can actually restimulate old wounds and continue to remind you of negative emotions associated with someone in your past. Discarding or storing these reminder objects will usually bring some relief.

2. **Purge your anger.** You may still have unresolved anger at a parent, an old work associate, or an ex. It is okay to feel some anger, but if you don't deal with that anger constructively, you can't let go of the past. Try writing a really angry letter to that person—and then throw it away. This really works!

3. **Don't blame yourself.** Whatever happened in the past to create hurt that you hold on to, don't blame yourself. Instead, blame the relationship or situation. When you can really forgive yourself by saying things like, "I was young. I didn't know any better. I handled it as best I could at the time," you will be able to finally let go of the baggage associated with the past.

4. **Don't repeat the pattern.** When we carry old wounds, we sometimes behave in the present as if that relationship or situation is still going on. Instead, be in the present, look at your current relationship and situation, and change your behavior to fit the way things actually are right now.

5. **Ask for help.** If you are really feeling distressed, angry, or upset, or if you feel like the past is preventing you from moving on, I strongly encourage you to seek out the assistance of a counselor or therapist. Another person's perspective can really help in these situations—and will help you be happier and more open in your marriage.

Rule is a fun, simple, and highly effective way to do that. Here's a review of what we covered in this chapter:

- Daily briefing talk has been shown to create more happiness in a marriage.
- Practice the Ten-Minute Rule every day. Talk with your spouse about anything other than kids, work, or household tasks and responsibilities.
- The four areas you need to know about your spouse if you want a truly great relationship are: best friends, current stressors, life dreams, and basic values.
- Learn to ask great questions. Ask questions that require more than one-word answers, and often start with "what" or "why." Ask questions about specific people or events that are important to your spouse. Ask personal questions.
- Practice active listening. This means making eye contact, showing with your body language that you are attentive, and focusing your mind so you don't interrupt or get distracted.
- Relationship talk is not the same as daily briefing talk.
- Relationship talk has the effect of making women feel more connected, intimate, and amorous. It is an aphrodisiac for women.
- Research also shows that too much relationship talk has a *negative* effect on husbands, who report feeling less happy in the marriage when there's too much relationship talk. Men often associate relationship talk with relationship *problems*.

- When men talk about the relationship, they often discuss events and objects. Women engage in relationship talk differently, focusing on emotions and people.
- Miscommunication and unpacked baggage from your past are two obstacles that can get in the way of good, healthy communication with your spouse.
- Unpacking baggage with your spouse—telling him or her about old hurts, fears, or patterns you'd like to change—is a great occasional topic for the Ten-Minute Rule, and will bring you and your spouse closer together.

4

IMPLEMENT CHANGE

Take risks to reduce boredom and keep things fresh.

———

You have learned that to take your marriage from good to really great, you need to have realistic expectations, you need to do and say simple things to keep your spouse happy, and you need to have daily briefings so you can really get to know your partner. Once you know and understand how to put these three steps into practice, you are ready for the next step. Hang on, because this one promises to be fun and very exhilarating. The fourth step to achieving a truly great marriage is to implement change in order to reduce marital boredom and keep your relationship fresh and exciting. My research and clinical experience show that you need to shake things up a bit if you want your marriage to move from hum-drum to fun, and from good to really great.

In this chapter, I will talk about the top-two reasons mar-riages hit what I call a "happiness plateau": (1) falling into a re-lationship rut and (2) letting passion and sexuality fade. I hear these two complaints repeatedly. The great news is that both issues are easy to resolve by making small changes in your be-havior. I will show you practical ways to make these changes so you can see immediate results. You will learn how to try new behaviors to introduce freshness into your marriage. The goal here is to liven things up and reintroduce fun, excitement, sur-prise, and a little bit of fire and mystery into your relationship. By working through this step, you and your spouse will re-member why you chose each other in the first place.

TWO KINDS OF CHANGE

There are really two types of change that you need to imple-ment in your relationship to prevent marital boredom and keep your relationship fresh. The first is the type of change that gently knocks your partner off balance, makes him or her respond in a new way, and shakes up the routine. I liken this first type of change to the moves of a great baseball pitcher. He can strike out most batters with his 90-mph fastball. But if that's all he throws, sooner or later batters will get used to his lightning and hit his pitches every time. However, if he can mix things up with a changeup, a curveball, and maybe a slider, the batters won't know what to expect and it keeps them guessing. It also makes them better hitters because they have to pay attention and learn new ways to react in the moment. That's the idea behind the first type of change. You want to take away your spouse's "automatic response" factor so he or she will be compelled to respond to you and each situation in a fresh way.

The second type of change is the kind that introduces mystery and novelty into the marriage. Although it is more dramatic and requires more risk on your part, it will have the effect of astonishing your partner. The purpose of this type of change is to reignite the flame, spark more passion, and liven up the sexiness in your marriage. Step back and remember when your relationship was new. You probably were surprised or impressed by everything your partner said or did. Do you remember when intimate dinners for two led to long talks? Do you recall when each weekend was spent sharing and experiencing a new activity together? Maybe you can recall the first few times you tried to blend your friends and family together so your lives intersected. Remember the thrill of sex and the warm feeling you got first thing in the morning when you felt him or her by your side under the sheets? Those were the good old days, right? And now you're wondering, "Where did that all go?"

Even though you feel slightly bored and the passion and sexiness may have dwindled in your relationship to a nonexistent level, you can change this, I promise! By getting out of your relationship rut and re-creating passion and sexuality in your marriage, you will see your marriage change from good to really great.

RELATIONSHIP RUT

It is very common for a relationship to fall into a rut. It becomes routine and humdrum, and partners start feeling as though they are missing all of the good things that make relationships fun and exciting. Bear in mind that you and your partner don't have to be fighting or not having sex to be in a rut. A rut comes about when you can't quite remember why you are married to each other. In a relationship rut, there may not be anything seriously wrong with your marriage; it has just become boring, routine, and monotonous. Most relationships go through periods like this, but if it goes on for years, it can become a problem and lead to unhappiness.

In my study, we asked all the couples the following question: "During the past month, how often did you feel that your marriage was in a rut (or falling into a rut), where you felt like you were doing the same thing all the time and rarely doing exciting things together as a couple?" Over 42 percent of all the husbands and wives felt that their marriages were in a rut (or falling into a rut). We found it to be a very common complaint. However, here's the red flag: I also found that couples who felt as though their marriage was in a rut year after year were significantly *less* happy each year they were interviewed. In fact, I found that chronic relationship ruts (those that persist for years on end) are an accurate predictor of marital unhappiness and spousal distress nine years later. In relationships where the spouses characterized the marriage as being in a rut in the seventh year, the spouses' happiness was more likely to have decreased at year sixteen. The lesson for

> ### DID YOU KNOW...
>
> My research suggests a strong connection between marital happiness and staying out of a relationship rut. Consider this: 78 percent of the happy couples in my long-term study say they "rarely or never" feel as if they are in a relationship rut.

you? Getting your relationship out of a rut *now* will increase your chances of happiness—*now and years into the future.*

Let's look at three factors that cause a relationship rut, and learn simple, concrete behavioral changes you can make to reduce boredom and increase happiness.

Cause #1: Living parallel lives.

Why the Rut Happens

First, relationships can fall into a rut because the two partners are living almost parallel lives. What does this mean? The husband and wife feel as if they are working together well in terms of raising the kids, maintaining the house, saving money, and planning for the future. In other words, they are both progressing along toward the same life goals. However, they are not crossing paths on the way from point A to point B. Rather, it's almost as if they are moving forward toward the same destination, but on parallel tracks.

When children and the juggling of work and family come

into the marriage picture, one partner may be busy taking the kids to school, helping with kids' homework, organizing social events, and working outside the home. The other partner may be trying to start a new business, coaching the kids' sports teams, and golfing on the weekend. They are each so busy doing what they are doing separately that they just don't take time to cross paths, which keeps their lives from intersecting in meaningful ways. They continue to do the same or routine things because it is what keeps the family or couple going. But when this happens, the partners may bore each other or even feel slightly estranged when they do spend time together.

I can't tell you how many times I have talked to patients who were anxious before going on a five-day trip with their spouses. They worried they wouldn't have much to talk about and do with their spouses for such a long period of time. They hadn't really spent time together, just the two of them, in years! Does this sound like you? Believe me when I say it is very common for this type of relationship rut to occur— because people's lives are so busy these days, and it takes both partners to manage jobs, a home, and kids, not to mention a social life, extended family, and life issues that arise to complicate matters, such as health and finances.

How to Get Out of the Rut

Keep that image of the parallel tracks in your mind. Each of you may be doing a really good job in the marriage, but in order to feel happier and more interested, you have to change direction slightly so your paths will intersect from time to time. To do this, *you need to slow down.* Yes, we are very busy as individuals. We take on too many responsibilities and tasks, and we put our relationships on the back burner. You know, you think your relationship will still be there when you finish your next deadline, after you climb the corporate ladder, or as soon as you attend to the needs of your elderly dad. But your marriage isn't something that waits in the background until you are ready to deal with it. In order for you and your spouse to get out of the relationship rut, just slow down and take a look at what is happening now—right now. Don't wait until tomorrow. Take time today to notice what your partner is doing. Take time to appreciate him or her. Think about how your spouse's contribution makes a positive difference in your family's life.

Here's a little exercise I use to help people see if they are charging ahead too fast on a parallel track, and not slowing down to notice their partners. I ask a wife or husband: "Did you notice what your partner was wearing this morning?" More than half of the time, neither spouse can remember. Try this: Tomorrow morning, slow down your morning routine and notice what your partner is wearing. This small behavioral change resets your brain to change speed—much like an off-speed pitch subtly trains the batter to focus. When you and your spouse make a habit of slowing down, noticing, and appreciating each other, you will find that the two of you naturally start to connect and your lives start to intersect more. You will take more interest in each other's activities. You will find new topics to talk about. You may even make plans to do something together—just the two of you. Watch the almost miraculous ripple effect this small behavioral change—

THE LOVE DOCTOR'S RELATIONSHIP-RUT QUIZ

Find out whether your marriage is in a rut by taking the following quiz. For each statement, circle TRUE or FALSE.

1. **TRUE FALSE** I can remember when my partner last said or did something that genuinely surprised me.

2. **TRUE FALSE** Our daily routines together vary from month to month.

3. **TRUE FALSE** We have gone on a date together, just the two of us, in the last four months.

4. **TRUE FALSE** My spouse always notices changes in my appearance or things I've purchased for the house.

5. **TRUE FALSE** We've gone on a vacation together, just the two of us, in the last two years.

6. **TRUE FALSE** My spouse and I are willing to change our habits and routine.

7. **TRUE FALSE** We have tried a new hobby or activity together in the last year.

8. **TRUE FALSE** My spouse and I switch roles from time to time in our relationship, such as bill payer, thank-you-note sender, or bathroom cleaner.

9. **TRUE FALSE** I often remember what my spouse wears when he/she leaves the house in the morning.

10. **TRUE FALSE** Most of the new, fresh, exciting experiences I have occur when I am with my spouse.

SCORING: Add up the number of "False" responses circled. Here's what your score indicates.

8–10 **Grand canyon.** You and your spouse are in a pretty significant relationship rut. Although this relationship rut isn't necessarily bad for the marriage short-term, it does have a negative impact on *individual* happiness. Fortunately, it takes only a small, simple behavioral change to get out of a canyon-size rut. Get started this week and watch how quickly things start to feel fresh and different.

4–7 **Roadside ditch.** If you always keep one wheel in that ditch, you and your spouse won't be able to get anywhere else. If you're on the low side of this score, it indicates you are doing a decent job keeping things in your marriage from getting old and stale. If you're on the higher end, it indicates that there's too much boredom in your marriage, and you will benefit greatly from trying some of the action steps I recommend in this chapter. Try one small behavioral change a week and watch what happens.

0–3 **Carriage track.** Like carriage tracks in a muddy country road, your relationship behavior creates a noticeable pattern that could become deeper and more set over time. However, this score indicates that you and your spouse are terrific at keeping each other interested, surprised, happy, and feeling appreciated and noticed. Keep up the great work, and don't let your shallow tracks turn into deeper ruts.

slowing down—has on your marriage. Slowing down creates interest and combats boredom.

I love this story told by Patti, a kindergarten teacher and one of the happy wives from my marriage study. It is a perfect illustration of how "slowing down" helps you see your spouse more clearly.

In my kindergarten class, we use the "freeze moment." At random moments in the middle of class, I'll say "Freeze!" All the kids stop whatever they're doing and freeze. The kids get hysterical when they see someone is under the table, another is at the window, someone else is grabbing his friend's markers. It's just a fun way for me to gain control and help the students refocus. But I kind of have a version of this I use with Max [her husband]. Sometimes he'll say something to me that's really perceptive, and I'll think, "Freeze." I kind of take a mental snapshot of that moment. Or sometimes I'll do it to myself when I've said something snippy to him or ignored him, which I instantly regret. I like to freeze these small moments in my mind, both good and bad, because they really give me something to think about. I don't want to be a zombie in my marriage—just trudging through. I think that kind of effort we put into it has helped keep our marriage stable.

Cause #2: Lacking balance between rational and fun.

Why the Rut Happens

Another reason a relationship rut may occur is because people forget that marriage is not just about caring for children and creating a secure and stable home. It is also about fun and play. To be truly happy, you need to strike a balance between stability and whimsy. The happy couples in my study characterized their partners as fun to be around, people they enjoyed spending time with. Too often, after a marriage has matured, partners tend to look to outside friends for fun and entertainment, and to their spouse for security and stability. Similar to Cause #1, living parallel lives, this lack of balance between the rational and the playful seems to occur because couples get too caught up in the day-to-day management of the home, job, and family, and they make play a secondary priority. In a happy marriage, you need a balance of both.

How to Get Out of the Rut

Okay, so you and your partner don't have as much fun as you used to. This is an easy one to change. You just need to pepper your month with one or two fun activities that get you laughing, relaxing together, or playing. If you have kids, it's pretty simple to come up with play. A family game of volleyball in the pool, backyard miniature golf, or kickball will get you and your spouse playing and acting young again. How about a spousal snowball fight? Renting a comedy DVD or playing cards is also great. You can have fun as a family or just the two of you, as long as you and your partner laugh and play together.

Scientists who research relationships have shown that humor and laughter have wide-ranging social benefits. In a variety of studies, researchers have found that laughter helped medical professionals cope better with their difficult jobs. It increased communication in workplace settings. It has also been shown to reduce stress, bind people together socially, and boost mood. In other words, laughing with your spouse will make you feel closer, work and live more easily together, and be happier.

My patient, Amy, recently told me this charming story about her husband, Wally, when they were visiting his family in New York City over Thanksgiving.

Wally shook me awake in the middle of the night. It was 3:00 a.m. I thought, oh no, one of his parents has had a heart attack. But he was smiling and told me to get up and throw on some warm clothes—we were going out. We had to tiptoe around his parents' apartment. He wouldn't tell me where we were going. We took a cab to the Museum of Natural History where there were crowds of people, with vendors selling hot chocolate. It's where they blow up the giant balloons the night before the Macy's Thanksgiving Day parade! We watched them inflate the giant Shrek with this huge loud blower, and every balloon had about ten people holding it down with ropes. Wally's parents used to bring him there when he was a kid, and he wanted me to see it. It was so spontaneous and unusual for Wally, but it made me feel so happy and young and in love with him again.

DID YOU KNOW...

Laughter activates the release of dopamine in the brain, which reinforces pleasure-seeking behaviors and influences our happiness. It also stimulates the release of endorphins, opiate substances that make us feel good.

You don't have to do something as spectacularly creative as Wally did to add more fun. But look at what an effect it had on Amy.

If you happen to be married to a serious sort, don't worry. There are other ways to play and have fun. Plan an activity you both get a kick out of, whether it's going to the horse races, playing tennis, or doing the Sunday crossword puzzle together. The idea here is to lighten up. You don't have to do a lot of elaborate planning or change your routine all that much. Just inject some levity into the relationship to bring more balance into your marriage and counteract the same-old, same-old boredom.

Cause #3: Taking each other for granted.

Why the Rut Happens
The third reason husbands and wives fall into relationship ruts is because they begin to take each other for granted. In a typical marriage, each person starts adopting certain roles

over time, and they get entrenched in them. For example, the wife might always be the one to shop and cook. The husband might always be the one to find hotels and make travel arrangements. Next, things start to feel very predicable. Before long, he's coming home asking her what's for dinner without considering the fact that at the end of his wife's workday, she's had to shop, plan, and now prepare a meal. Meanwhile, she's asking him if the hotel will have an ocean view and a workout room, and whether he remembered to give the airlines her frequent-flier number. She doesn't consider the fact that it took her husband three hours on the Web to find a great hotel that would also fit with their child care schedule, budget, and her preferences. What's happening here is that both spouses make assumptions about their partner based on habit, routine, and preset roles. They don't check in with their spouse to find out how the other is feeling, they don't notice actual changes in their spouse, and then they start taking it for granted that their partner will behave the same. Boring! This type of attitude can also build resentment and be infuriating—not what you want in a marriage—so you need to bring it to an end by changing some behaviors.

How to Get Out of the Rut

To help you and your partner stop taking each other for granted, you need to knock your partner gently off balance. It is important that you do surprising things that make your married life less predictable. Every relationship needs excitement now and then, so take some time to intentionally break up the monotony. In my study, I found that when spouses reported that they engaged in new or exciting activities with their partners, they were happier in their marriages.

Here is a story from Stacy, one of the wives in my long-term study.

No joke, you could set an atomic clock by my husband. He's home at 5:30, in his green track suit by 5:45, and watching TV by 6:00. In between, he sniffs around the kitchen to see what's for dinner, inquires if there's anything new with the kids, and grabs a diet soda before heading to the family room. Meanwhile, I'm in the kitchen daydreaming about salsa lessons and running away to Ecuador as I accidentally overcook dinner! Don't get me wrong—I love Jim. And I kind of love his rock-solid stability. But I'm starting to feel restless, and I wonder if it will always be this way.

Stacy's story is incredibly common. We love our spouses, but . . . In the business world, such behaviors can be really damaging. In fact, the best companies get their employees to engage in risk-taking and thinking outside of the box so they don't get too set in their ways, and so they will be flexible enough to meet new business challenges creatively, effectively, and quickly. Employees who are too comfortable with the status quo and the same way of working and approaching problems can become resistant to new ideas, and are less able to adapt to new circumstances (such as changing market conditions, technologies, or competitors). The same is true for marriage. You need to shake things up a bit to help your spouse

THE LOVE DOCTOR'S TIPS FOR GENTLY KNOCKING
YOUR PARTNER OFF BALANCE

Here are some ways to gently upset the status quo in your marriage so you and your partner can step out of your humdrum routine and get out of a relationship rut.

If he always turns on the TV after dinner, try . . .

. . . making a midweek dinner reservation and enjoying a long meal together.

. . . taking the kids to a golf driving range or batting cage after dinner.

. . . renting a romantic movie to watch together at night.

. . . inviting him for a walk, or to watch the sunset with you.

If she always works on Saturdays, try . . .

. . . planning a Saturday brunch with favorite friends.

. . . waking up first and bringing her breakfast in bed.

. . . telling her you've made time to help her with that gardening project.

. . . bringing her flowers in the middle of her work session.

Other ideas:

• **Switch roles:** cooking, washing the car, shopping, chauffeuring kids.

- **Propose something new:** a class to take together, a museum tour, a household project.

- **Behave differently:** meet for lunch during the workday, play hooky from work and hike to a waterfall together, eat vegetarian for a week.

- **Share roles:** go food shopping together, rake the yard together, go to your child's sports practice together.

learn new behaviors if you want your marriage to go in new and interesting directions, instead of moving along in the same old rut.

If we use Stacy's example, here are some very simple ways she could introduce new elements into the marital routine that would have the effect of gently knocking Jim off balance and waking him up. Stacy might have the family watch a rented movie or play team Scrabble at 6:00—over pizzas that she had delivered. It sounds insignificant, but I emphasize the importance of *small acts that shake things up*. In this case, eating with the kids, watching a movie, and/or playing a game alters the status quo and upsets the regular routine. It would get Jim focused on Stacy and the kids and relieve Stacy from her evening cooking job. Next stop, salsa lessons and a Caribbean cruise? You never know! Notice in the above example that I am not talking about changing *Jim*. Trying to make your spouse different is a big Love Doctor no-no. Instead, I am just talking about implementing small changes to keep your partner a little off balance.

FADING PASSION AND LACKLUSTER SEX

The number-one question I'm consistently asked about relationships from patients, students, and radio/TV listeners is: "Where has all the passion and romance gone in my relationship? Is there something wrong with my marriage?" Here is a recent example:

> Dear Dr. Terri: My wife and I have been together for five years and the romance and fireworks we experienced during the first few years have become a distant memory. We don't fight, and we still love each other, but the passion is gone. We don't seem to have fun together anymore either. The spark has fizzled. I once thought I had the most amazing relationship in the world, but now I feel like we're just like a lot of other couples I know. I don't want to live without sex, and I'm beginning to wonder if this is the right relationship for me. Should I consider leaving and trying to find someone else?

The decline in passionate love in your marriage says nothing about you or your partner. It doesn't mean that you are in a bad relationship. In this next part of Step 4, we will find out about the second kind of change that transforms good marriages into dynamic, exciting marriages. As mentioned earlier, this one is a more dramatic type of change, where you introduce *new elements* into the mix to stir things up. This second type of change will result in a significant emotional shift between you and your partner. In other words, your husband or wife will sit upright and really take notice. The idea is to get your spouse to look at you with new eyes.

There is a great deal of research showing that passionate love and sex do indeed decline in frequency and intensity over the course of a marriage. It is a natural part of any relationship. Most of the couples in my long-term study report that sexual frequency declines over the first several years of marriage, especially as children are born. Often when I share this information with couples, they feel disappointed and let down. If you're also feeling this way, here's some good news. You can re-create, intensify, and reignite both passion and sex by trying new activities and trying on new behaviors.

As you read through this part of Step 4, keep in mind that both passionate love and enjoyable sex are extremely critical to making you and your partner really happy. Many people confuse passion and sex; they are not the same. Passionate love is a strong emotion, not a physical act. It is a feeling that may include a powerful desire to be with your partner. It also may involve a desire to be with your partner sexually or produce sexual arousal, but passionate love itself does not mean sex. Sex is the *behavior* that occurs between two partners, which encompasses a wide range of activities and sexual contact. As you'll learn, passionate love and sex are incredibly interconnected, and there are interesting differences in how males and females relate to passion and sex in order to achieve emotional connection. Once you understand these differences, you will be better equipped to implement targeted behavioral changes to get your mate's passion burning and sexual desire recharged. The happy couples in my study have learned how to add mystery and novelty to their marriages to reignite the passion and spice up sexuality—and you can too.

PASSIONATE LOVE

Let's begin by understanding passionate love. Passion or passionate love is a strong emotion or feeling, which has a physiological foundation. Most people experience passionate love when they connect with a partner emotionally and are intensely attracted to that person. If you close your eyes and think back, you can probably remember that powerful good feeling that affected you physiologically. Remember how your heart rate increased rapidly, you felt a rush of adrenaline go through your entire body, and you became aware of an overwhelming desire to be with him or her? Studies by Elaine Hatfield and Ellen Berscheid, two psychologists who did a lot of research on passionate love in romantic relationships, discovered that passionate love includes two factors: (1) physiological arousal—the kind you feel in your body—and (2) understanding that your partner is the cause of that arousal, either by thinking about or being with him or her. These two factors combine to form passionate love.

The level of passionate love is high early in a relationship because everything is new and exciting. When you learn interesting and novel information about your partner every day, it fuels the passion. Plus, in the early stages of a relationship, you idealize your partner and see him or her through rose-colored glasses. You actually ignore or minimize your partner's faults or any undesirable information that isn't flattering.

He snores? You don't even notice it! She's messy? You don't even see the clothes you're stepping over on the floor! She laughs at everything? You think it's sweet! Why? Because passionate love and romance are enhanced by these idealized glorifications of your partner.

As time goes by, though, the rose-colored glasses come off and you begin to see the imperfections that every partner, every person has. You begin to really know your partner in every way—what he or she eats at a restaurant, thinks about politics, and enjoys doing on a Sunday afternoon. This information increases *companionate* love, the love that is characterized by support, intimacy, and friendship, but it also weakens feelings of passionate love. There are simply no more big mysteries.

Most couples go through this. In fact, research confirms that the majority of married couples fail to maintain the urgent longing, passion, and desire for each other that was there at the beginning of the relationship. The decrease in passionate love can sometimes be quite rapid. Psychologist Ted Huston studied married couples and found that after only eighteen months of being married, passionate love decreased to 50 percent of what it was when the couples were first married. The critical point here is that your relationship is not in trouble when you experience the decline. Instead, this decline in passionate love is an inevitable part of being in a long-term relationship.

However, there is good news at the end of the love tunnel. The first piece of good news is that at the same time passionate love declines, companionate love, which is characterized by friendship, intimacy, and commitment, actually *increases* over the course of a relationship. Companionate love, as my research and that of others has found, is what actually keeps couples together over time. As a relationship researcher, I am always curious to know what couples feel is "the secret" to a long marriage. I love asking elderly couples who have a few decades of marriage under their belts, "What's kept you married for so long?" Without fail, they report being great friends and companions. The feeling of knowing another person so well and fitting so comfortably together, like a glove on a hand, is really what makes companionate love such a powerful and profound force. The happy couples in my long-term study who have been married longer than fifteen years report both a high level and a *steady increase* in companionate love over time.

The second bit of good news is that when passionate love does start to decline, it can be reignited by implementing simple, small changes to your relationship. Passionate love and companionate love can occur together—all it takes is creativity, time, and a mutual desire to try. Couples are always delighted to discover that it's easier than they thought it would be—not to mention, fun! Remember, passion is essential to any long-term romantic relationship. It is needed to take your marriage from good to really great.

Before we get to the topic of sex and how it is related to passionate love, let's pinpoint six simple ways to recharge the passion in your marriage. I have translated current relationship research, my own and that of other experts, into these six easy-to-implement behavioral changes. Each tip is designed to give your partner a jolt—large or small—that gets emotions flowing freely between you again, just like when you first met. I promise the tips will work for you, just as they have worked for countless others.

THE LOVE DOCTOR'S SIX WAYS TO REIGNITE PASSION

1. *Engage in new activities.* Doing novel activities with your partner enables you both to reexperience that original emotional state you had when you were newly acquainted. Novelty and excitement were part of the recipe that created the passionate love you felt at the beginning of your relationship. Your body will still feel physiological arousal, even if your logical mind knows you are "tricking" it. Go deep-sea fishing on a bracing afternoon. Learn to ski with your spouse. Swing your pelvis in an African dance and drumming workshop. One wife in my marriage study planned a treasure hunt for her husband that took him all around the city until he ended up at an ice-skating rink. They had the best time with each other doing this outrageously different activity. Unique, unexpected experiences you share together will spice up your love life and add romantic flavor to the relationship.

2. *Get away from it all.* Try taking a mini-vacation, just the two of you. Your getaway together should last at least one night and two days. It is important that you go somewhere that interests both of you, where you can create new memories and spend unpressured time together. You

don't have to go far from home, just a place where you can spend some quality time together. My husband and I once went one mile away and checked into a local hotel for a romantic break. We felt as if we were in another state once we checked in. The whole idea is to change your surroundings. If you can, turn your cellphones and computers off during your romantic excursion. Studies show this is particularly important for women, since women feel more passionate when they are away from the other pressures in their lives. I know this may be more challenging for couples who have small children, but ask a relative to watch the kids and try to remember that you are investing in your relationship now and into the future.

3. *Seek arousal-producing activities.* This is my favorite suggestion, but it is not what you are imagining! Several psychology studies show that if you do activities with your partner that produce brain chemicals associated with arousal, this arousal can get transferred to your private, intimate relationship. Scientists say this transferred arousal gets "misattributed" to your partner. Again you are, in a sense, fooling your brain chemistry. The two factors— physiological arousal and the belief that your partner is the cause of the arousal (even if she or he isn't)—combine to form passionate love. Activities that create fear (e.g., rollercoaster rides or scary movies) or that cause an upsurge in the "feel-good" brain chemicals (e.g., working out or vigorous hiking) actually increase passionate love, as long as you do them with your partner. It's easy and it works! The

arousal produced through another activity transfers to your relationship and partner, and you will both experience an upsurge in passionate feelings.

A forty-one-year-old female patient of mine, an antiques dealer, complained that her marriage lacked pizzazz. She loved her husband, who was a businessman. She described him as a great friend whom she could talk to about everything. They had two kids, and both worked hard at their jobs. But at night they would fall into bed exhausted from the day. "Passion," she said, "is the last thing on either of our minds." When I mentioned to her how physical arousal in the presence of someone you love gets easily transformed into passionate feelings, she exclaimed, "You know, that's really funny you say that, because after I've had a really vigorous workout at the Y, I often have these surges of love for him. It's a time when I often will send him a text." I suggested that, if possible, she take her husband on a shopping excursion to buy two pieces of exercise equipment to put in their basement so they could work out side by side. They purchased an elliptical machine for her and a weight bench with free weights for him. A month later she thanked me. "We committed to working out together three times a week and I can't tell you how it's improved things. It's like we're really connected. There's a lot more hugging, fondness, kissing, and lovemaking."

4. *Get reacquainted as friends.* You can also keep the passion alive in your relationship by nurturing a friendship with your spouse. As we talked about in Step 3, when you learn new information or qualities about your partner, it brings you closer together. But it also invites passion. You can reacquaint yourself with your partner by playing a board game together, such as Scrabble or Trivial Pursuit. You also might want to attend a marriage enrichment workshop together. Passion can be re-created, especially for women, when the two of you clarify your expectations and rules for your relationship at these workshops.

5. *Touch your partner.* Remember that passionate love is an intense good feeling that affects you physiologically. You can re-create this underlying physiological arousal through touch or another physical connection like kissing. Holding hands or practicing other small endearments, such as a neck rub or a surprise hug from behind, keep romance alive. These are necessary for couples to feel physically bonded, which is important to passionate love. Studies show that people feel better and more connected to their partners when they touch frequently: hold hands, hug, cuddle, and kiss.

6. *Find a new way to say those three little words.* At the beginning of a relationship, most partners express their feelings and strong emotions for each other. Another way to refuel the passion in your relationship is to express those same emotions now, but in a unique and different way. Be sure to let your spouse know you are thinking of him or her, and that even during your busy day, you care. This can be

TIP

Ever notice how passionate you feel after a spin on the dance floor with your spouse at a wedding or bar mitzvah? Dance is an activity that gives you a lot of bang for your buck in terms of reigniting passion in your marriage. Dance allows you to touch each other, try a fresh activity together, and produce physical arousal that can get transferred to your spouse.

extremely exciting and romantic. Do it in a way you have not done it before. Over the last ten years, I have been analyzing the ways people say *I love you* to each other. I have heard many complicated and expensive ways to do this, such as renting a billboard on a highway or making an announcement at a basketball game. But simple, inexpensive, and unexpected approaches are the best ingredients for re-creating passion.

Sexuality

So what does sex have to do with romance and passionate love? Put simply, a lot! As mentioned earlier, passionate love and sex are not the same thing—and for some people, sex need not even involve or be related to passionate love. Remember, passion is a *feeling,* sex is a *behavior.* But for most people, passionate love and sex are integrally connected, and

THE LOVE DOCTOR'S TOP-TEN WAYS
TO SAY "I LOVE YOU"

1. Send an email or text message out of the blue: "Here's just one reason I love you . . ."
2. Put a greeting card in the mail. Mail from a spouse is always a surprise.
3. Slip a handmade coupon on his or her pillow—for a foot massage from you, performing a hated chore, washing the car, etc.
4. Make a reservation at the restaurant where you had your first date.
5. Make your spouse a CD collection of the music you first listened to and loved together.
6. Make your partner his or her favorite dinner or dessert.
7. Read a morning love poem to your partner while he or she is still in bed.
8. Have your favorite photo of you two framed or transferred onto a coffee mug.
9. Send his or her parents a thank-you note for bringing your beloved into the world.
10. Buy a DVD on massage and tell your spouse to schedule an appointment.

the strong desire and feeling of passionate love for one's partner can lead to sex or sexual contact with each other. While passionate love is a strong emotion connected to physiological arousal, sex is a group of behaviors, actions, and experiences that allow the expression of one's passionate love feelings.

> ## DID YOU KNOW...
>
> Researchers at the University of Albany (Susan M. Hughes, Marissa A. Harrison, and Gordon G. Gallup, Jr.) found gender differences in the importance and type of kissing in relationships. Men tended to kiss as a means to an end—to gain sexual favors or to reconcile a relationship. Men also said they were happy to have sex without kissing. In contrast, women said they kiss to establish and monitor the status of their relationship, and to assess and periodically update the level of commitment on the part of a partner. They also place more emphasis on kissing, and most will not engage in sex without kissing.

These behaviors may include, but are not restricted to, kissing, oral sex, anal sex, touching a partner's body, or sexual intercourse. Healthy sexual behaviors for married couples are consensual, nonexploitive, and allow spouses to physically bond and connect to each other.

Biologically speaking then, both passionate love and sex have an underlying physiological component. But psychologically, there is much more to this connection. First, the feelings of passionate love may lead to healthy sexual behaviors as an expression of those strong emotions. Conversely, but just as likely to occur, when healthy sexual behaviors are experienced, they can lead to feelings of strong passionate love.

What's important in happy marriages, however, is that you have to have both. Based on my research, it's abundantly clear

DID YOU KNOW...

Is there a connection between marital happiness and good sex? My findings suggest there is. Consider this: 75 percent of the happy couples in my long-term study say they are satisfied with their sexual relationship. Only 9 percent of the happy couples mention that they are very upset with their sex life together.

that if you want to take your marriage from good to great, you need to have both passionate love *and* sex. It turns out that the quantity of sex is not as important as the quality. In fact, a whopping 75 percent of happy couples in my study reported that sex became less frequent over time. However, that same percentage—75 percent—also said that they were satisfied with their sex life. Why? Because eight out of ten happy couples felt that their sexual activity, even if less frequent, was just as enjoyable or *more* enjoyable than when they were first together. Quality, not quantity, is the name of the game. That's great news for all those couples out there who worry that having less sex means something is wrong.

But the big idea here is that you need to have a connection to each other, emotionally and physically, in order to experience a really fantastic marriage. In the earlier part of the chapter, I gave you tried-and-true tips on how to reignite passionate love in your marriage and regain that emotional connection. Now let's learn how to recharge your sex life and spice up that physical connection.

What Happens to Sex Over Time?

In my long-term study of marriage, the frequency of sex among all couples significantly declined over time, as reported by both husbands and wives. The approach and meaning of that decline, however, varied from spouse to spouse and was not necessarily related to sexual satisfaction. For some couples, having sex twice a month feels right, and both partners experience the sex as highly satisfying. For others, once a week is the minimum for their happiness. People differ in how often they want, need, and desire sex in order to be sexually satisfied. However, the happy couples in my study let their spouses know that sex is important to them, and they talk to each other about how much they need to feel content.

One of the positive findings that came out of my research is that sex is alive and well in American couples. Among happy couples, good, satisfying sex was a common theme. Here's but one example. I could cite dozens like this one!

Corrine and Jose have known each other since high school and got married young. They have four children. Corrine runs a child care business out of their home, and Jose is an electrician. Two interesting things occurred when they came together to discuss their personal expectations for marriage at year sixteen. First, there was quite a bit of laughter, joking, and playfulness with each other.

Both husband and wife made jokes about how each other's sexual needs and desires were rated as a "very important" expectation in their marriage, but still didn't get the ranking as number one or two in the list of sixteen common marriage expectations. They both admitted that sex was less frequent now than in the early years of their marriage, but Corrine added, "It's way more fun now, though. Partly because I don't have to worry about getting pregnant anymore [they spoke about Jose's vasectomy earlier] and partly because he knows what I like so well at this point." Jose agreed, but seemed more embarrassed by the subject. "She's great—in bed and in all other ways." [More laughter and big smiles.]

With Corrine and Jose, one could almost feel an electrical charge in the room. That sensation in the presence of happily married couples is quite common—and as I have also found, quite possible to regain.

Regardless of how often you would like sex in your marriage, it is also important to understand that men and women are different when it comes to sex and love. And when I say different, I don't mean who wants more or less sex in a relationship. Instead, one of the things I have confirmed about people's beliefs from my marriage study and my patients over the years is that there are gender differences in the link between physical closeness (sex) and emotional closeness (love).

Typically, women want and desire emotional closeness in order to feel sexual or to desire sexual intimacy with their partner. Conversely, men desire physical intimacy or sexuality in order to achieve emotional closeness. I found that among husbands, a key predictor of happiness and commitment to the marriage was establishing a particularly satisfying sexual relationship with their wives.

I am reminded of a poignant story from one of my patients regarding the role that these gender differences in sexuality played in their marriage. This couple experienced a miscarriage after six months of the wife's being pregnant. It was devastating to both spouses. The wife was feeling angry and depressed because her husband wanted to have sex with her soon after the miscarriage. The husband wanted to have sex, not to conceive another child, but to connect emotionally to his wife. He was using the physical intimacy of sexuality as a means to achieve emotional intimacy. Also, the husband viewed sex as a way to give his wife comfort and reassurance.

In contrast, the wife had no desire to have sex with her husband. She knew that she loved him, but she froze every time she even thought about being touched or being sexual. It wasn't until the wife expressed her feelings of loss and grief to her husband over time that she began to desire sex again. She needed to feel emotionally connected to him in order to experience sexual desire and feelings again.

When I pointed out to this patient the gender differences in the way she and her husband perceived sex—he as a way to get close to her again, and she as something she didn't want until she could resolve her feelings—it really helped her see how her husband was trying to heal himself and the relationship as well. He wasn't simply being needy or demanding.

How often do people in marriage typically have sex? The

answer to this question is, "It depends." The only fact we can be sure of is that married spouses have sex more often than single people. A recent study on sexuality by Edward Laumann and his colleagues at The University of Chicago found that, in general, married spouses have sex more often than single people because they have a sexual partner available to them more consistently. How often married couples have sex is related to a great many factors, including how satisfied the partners are with the relationship, age, hormone levels, current physical health, medications, depressive thoughts, and body image—to name a few. Any married couple knows that sex, at times, is a complex act. Is the timing right? Are you stressed out? Does he have something on his mind? Can you hear kids clanking around downstairs? Is it too hot? I could go on, but most people know there are plenty of things that can prevent sex from happening. Fortunately, most of these have easy fixes.

Why Sexual Feelings Fade—and How to Get Them Back

What if one of you is not interested in sex at all? Even though you love your spouse, you may not desire him or her sexually. Let's look at several possible reasons. The first step to finding workable solutions is to identify the underlying cause of your low libido.

Relationship Reasons

Do you feel disconnected from your spouse? Do you feel distant rather than close? You may lack the emotional intimacy you need. Revisit Step 3 in this book to pick up tips on how to regain closeness and emotional intimacy. Forgetting for a moment the pressure to have sex, ask yourself if you enjoy spending time with each other. If you answered no, then you may need to reconnect emotionally with your partner in order to respark your interest in sex. Here's what I would recommend to a patient in this situation. Plan a weekend away, just the two of you. But here is the key part: *The weekend should be free of all sex—no exceptions.* Instead, you should talk, cuddle, play, laugh, walk, read next to each other in bed, and so on. Leave all the distractions and responsibilities at home. When you communicate, spend time together, and share intimate thoughts again with your spouse, you will probably feel like having sex again. If the whole issue of sex feels too daunting, don't stress too much. You may want to see a sex or marital therapist to help you and your spouse work on the relationship in general, and the passion and sex in particular.

Psychological Reasons

Chronic stress and feeling depressed also can affect your desire to have sex with your spouse. Pressure at work or at home with family can lead to a reduced sex drive. Here is the first thing I would suggest. Try to identify what causes stress in your life by keeping a stress journal for a couple of weeks. Write down where you are and what you are doing when you feel extreme anxiety. Notice how these situations (deadlines, debt, family fighting, lack of privacy or time, etc.) and your reaction to each one affects your sex drive. Next, find a stress-reduction technique that works well for you, and make an effort to do it once a day. It might be deep breathing/meditation, vigorous aerobic exercise such as wind sprints or weight lifting, or even napping.

I am reminded of one of the happy couples in my study. The husband, Will, is an accountant. Here's what his wife said about him and how they have found a way to deal with his low sex drive caused by work stress.

> We have a good sex life—eight months of the year. But at the start of the year, he begins consulting with tax clients big-time. He does this all year round, but in January it starts to get real crazy. By April 15, Will is a basket case. Yes, he's a workaholic, but he insists it's the seasonal nature of his profession. I've gotten used to this. It used to just piss me off—that he could shut down emotionally, turn off his desire for me like a light switch, and leave me high and dry for four months. But I've come to realize that he's just too damn stressed to make love very often. I don't even ask him anymore. It's like he becomes a human calculator. I know it's really unhealthy for him, but I've learned to live with it. Now what I do is put in for my two-week vacation at work for the last week in April. We go away to someplace crazy each year—Tahiti, Costa Rica, Jamaica. It's basically to get our sex life going again. It's an accommodation I've learned to live with. We both have. Yes, I would say it pretty much works for us.

Most people who are depressed or feel withdrawn also lose interest in sex. Try to surround yourself with people who care about you, rather than facing the feelings alone. Also, talk to your physician about how to alleviate these feelings and get the depression under control. If you feel sad, alone, and hopeless, know that there are many well-researched and proven ways to turn your emotional state around. If you can get your stress and negative emotions under control, you may find that sex often feels less like a chore, and more like a vacation. Sex is also good for relieving stress, because during sex the feel-good hormones, such as oxytocin and endorphins, are released.

Physical Reasons

There are also multiple physical reasons for not desiring sex with your spouse. Hormonal imbalances affect the sexual drive of both women and men. Estrogen and testosterone are the hormonal building blocks of sexual desire. It is also very common for women to feel less sexual during the transition to menopause. Lack of sleep because of poor diet or hormonal fluctuations can also influence your interest in sex. Medical doctors report that certain medications and medical illnesses (e.g., diabetes, thyroid dysfunction, and circulation problems) can affect your interest in sex. Diabetes is the leading cause of impotence in men. In addition, for both men and women, blood flow is critical to facilitate sexual desire. See your doctor for a complete physical and ask her or him how to address any possible underlying physical causes of your low sex drive. Once you identify and treat the underlying physical conditions, your desire for sex can surprisingly reappear.

DID YOU KNOW...

If you have body-image self-consciousness during physical intimacy with your husband, it may have detrimental effects on your sexuality. A study in the *Journal of Sex Research* found that women who experienced the greatest degree of body-image self-consciousness during physical intimacy with a partner had less frequent sex, were less sexually assertive with partners, and reported more avoidance of sexual activity with a partner.

Body-image Reasons

Your body image is how you feel about yourself physically and how you think others see the shape, weight, and qualities of your body. Some people feel good about their bodies, while others don't. Bear in mind, though, that your body image may have no connection to what you actually look like. Someone who is very thin may look in the mirror and "see" a person who is much heavier. Another person may notice stretch marks all across her thighs, which no one else, especially a partner, has ever noticed. It doesn't matter how often your spouse compliments you or tells you that you look sexy. If you don't *feel* sexy, you may not have sexual desire.

Whether you recognize it or not, your body image has a huge effect on how you feel and act sexually. This is especially true for women. When you feel ashamed, self-conscious, and

THE LOVE DOCTOR'S TIPS
FOR A HEALTHY, POSITIVE BODY IMAGE

1. **Expand definitions of beauty.** Evaluate whether your notions of beauty include people from all cultures, ages, and different levels of physical ability. Ask yourself whether your notion of the perfect body is realistic for you.

2. **Have realistic expectations.** Set realistic expectations for what you want to see and feel with your own body. Go through magazines and television shows and ask questions about what is being portrayed. Accept and be okay with the fact that your body may look different from the media image. Besides, realistically, is any body free of cellulite, wrinkles, a few extra pounds, or some blemishes?

3. **Build confidence and self-esteem.** Remember that it is how you feel about yourself that's important—not the actual weight, height, or physical body mass that you possess. If you feel comfortable and confident in your body and about yourself, you will develop a positive body image.

4. **Practice self-affirmation.** Feeling good about your body must come from you! No matter how much your partner may say that your body is beautiful and sexy, it is self-affirmation that is important.

5. **Set new goals.** Find ways to feel good about your body and who you are. Exercise and a healthy diet are key. If you want, make a list of body goals that will motivate you to exercise and maintain a healthy diet.

anxious about your body, you can't enjoy sex with your partner. You don't even want your partner to see you naked for fear of rejection and humiliation. There is a great deal of research showing that body image is a significant influence on women's and men's desire for sex.

HOW TO ADD SPICE TO YOUR SEXUAL RELATIONSHIP

Just as with passionate love, there are several simple ways to add novelty and mystery to the sex in your marriage. I developed the list below to help couples improve their sexual relationship. I have shared it throughout the years to people in couples therapy and workshops, and the results can be stunning and immediate. Small changes in a relationship can respark the sexuality along with the passion.

Once again, remember that passionate love and sex are integrally tied. You can't implement simple changes to reignite the sexuality in your relationship without also making some changes to re-create the passionate love. Both connections (emotional and physical) are needed to take your marriage from good to really great.

Talk About Sex

It is important for couples to talk about their sex lives together. This can be helpful as well as physiologically arousing to both partners. You can discuss what makes your sex life exciting, your sexual fantasies, or what each of you might desire from your partner. A really good way to start this conversation is to remember back to the first several times you and your partner had sex. When you talk sex with your partner,

TIP FOR MEN

When you really get to know what your wife likes in bed, it will increase *your* sexual satisfaction as well as hers. Research findings published in the *Journal of Consulting and Clinical Psychology* reported that sexual satisfaction in both partners was associated with men's understanding of their female partners' sexual preferences.

focus on the positive. Instead of talking about what your partner *doesn't do* to excite you or turn you on, tell your partner what he or she *can do* to turn you on. For example, you might approach it from the angle that you would find it extremely erotic and arousing for him or her to initiate sex with you.

Develop Sex Signals

Some couples have their own secret or personal ways of telling each other they are interested in having sex. It may be a nod, a word, or even a certain sexy outfit. This sex signal is not evident to others; it is meant only for your spouse. This kind of secret language also adds mystery and suspense to your relationship, since you and your partner are the only ones who can understand and identify the signals.

Introduce Some New Ideas into Your Sexual Relationship

Novelty and newness are important to both passionate love and sexuality. It doesn't have to be a dramatic shift or change.

Some ideas: You can pick up bottles of scented massage oils, along with a book on massage tips, and take turns on each other. Play a romantic board game for couples. Wear a new or different article of clothing that your partner would love to see on you. Buy a sex toy. You also can change the place and situation for your lovemaking, which might stir things up a bit. So if you always have sex in the bedroom, try the kitchen, bathroom shower, or even your car.

Engage Sexual Fantasies

Sexual fantasies can be a healthy and natural part of a relationship. Some couples enjoy sexual fantasies as a way to create arousal or add excitement to their relationship. Other couples merely share their sexual fantasies through conversation, but don't explore them physically with each other. As long as a sexual fantasy or behavior doesn't lead to emotional or physical discomfort, conflict in the relationship, or problems in other aspects of their lives, it is perfectly acceptable and shouldn't be a source of concern. The most important thing to keep in mind is that if your partner's specific sexual fantasies are causing problems in your marriage or with your self-esteem, it isn't healthy to continue sharing or incorporating them into your relationship. Partners need to communicate and work together so that each feels good about their sexual relationship. This requires a willingness to listen and avoid making your spouse feel bad about having the fantasy in the first place.

Don't forget that a sexual fantasy can be just that: a thought or imagined sexual behavior. It doesn't have to imply

> **FANTASY TIP**
>
> Sharing a sexual fantasy requires trust. Never ridicule your partner's fantasy. If it makes you feel uncomfortable, simply tell your spouse your feelings.

that you or your partner is going to act on that fantasy or thought. You can, but you don't have to. Nonetheless, the decision to reveal a sexual fantasy can be dangerous and risky to a relationship. It is crucial that partners set ground rules and limitations before they share fantasies with each other. One very common boundary or limitation for many couples is that the fantasy should not include people you know or care about, especially if this is upsetting to one partner. Instead, be creative and have fun with it. Use your imagination. Make your partner the main feature of your sexual fantasy. What about a fantasy that uses a new sex toy you heard about from a friend?

Just Do It

The theory goes that getting those parts moving again will simply lead to more sex. Having sex makes you want to have it more. Two couples recently decided to kick-start their marriages by having sex every day. Charla and Brad Muller from Charlotte, North Carolina, managed to do it for an entire year, and wrote a book about their adventure entitled *365 Nights: A Memoir of Intimacy.* The other couple, Annie and

Douglas Brown from Boulder, Colorado, had sex 101 days in a row. They wrote a book called *Just Do It*. The take-away? The wives, Charla Muller and Annie Brown, both talked about how mandated physical intimacy created more emotional intimacy in their marriages. In a *New York Times* interview, Charla Muller said, "It required a daily kindness and forgiveness, and not being cranky or snarky, that I don't think either of us had experienced before." Will having sex a lot change your attitudes toward your spouse? It seemed to for these couples. You and your partner can try your own variation on this theme and you're likely to reap similar benefits.

STEP 4 TAKE-AWAYS

In this chapter you learned that implementing behavioral changes aimed at reducing marital boredom, reigniting passion, and recharging your sex life will bring a new level of excitement to your marriage. It's what happy couples in my study have learned how to do to keep things fresh. Here's a quick review of what we covered:

- There are two key reasons why marriages go flat: (1) falling into a relationship rut and (2) loss of passion and sexual excitement. Small changes can reinvigorate your marriage.
- Although relationship ruts are common among the married couples in my study, staying in a relationship rut was predictive of future unhappiness on the part of one or both spouses.

- There are three causes for a relationship rut: (1) living parallel lives and not having enough intersection in your separate routines; (2) not having a good balance between activities that promote stability and security and those that are whimsical, fun, and playful; and (3) taking each other for granted while allowing roles to get too firmly set.

- To get out of a relationship rut is simple. It requires that you make small changes in your behavior, which get you to slow down and remove the automatic response factor; you introduce novelty and fun into your marriage routine; and you knock your spouse gently off balance with new behaviors and responses.

- To be truly happy in a marriage, you need to have a healthy amount of both passionate love and sexual love. Passion is the emotion of love, and sex is the behavior that expresses it. Passion and sex both have a physiological basis, and are interconnected and interdependent.

- All couples in my study reported that passion, the emotion of romantic love, faded over time. However, companionate love, or the emotion of intimacy and friendship, actually *increased* over time for happy couples.

- A key finding from my study is that men tend to *get* emotional connection through sex, while women tend to *need* emotional connection to have sex.

- Passionate love is easy to reignite using simple techniques. Based on my own and others' relationship research, you can stimulate new behaviors, produce "love" chemicals in the brain, and retrigger old love emotions and body memories from the honeymoon period of your relationship.

- For the large majority of couples in my study, the frequency of sex declined over time. However, for the happiest couples, the *quantity* of sex was not predictive of marital unhappiness, while the *quality* of sex was.

- If you're not having sex at all, there may be four underlying reasons: (1) the emotional intimacy in your relationship is suffering and needs repair; (2) there could be psychological reasons such as chronic stress or depression, which may require professional help depending on severity; (3) there could be physical reasons such as hormone imbalances, illnesses such as diabetes, or side effects from medications, that require a physician's help; and (4) you or your partner may have a poor body image.

- There are easy, time-tested ways to jump-start your sex life and make it fresh and exciting. All it requires is your willingness to take some risks.

KEEP COSTS LOW, BENEFITS HIGH

Audit marriage behaviors to weed out
the unprofitable ones.

In the previous chapters, I have shared with you four simple steps you can use to take your marriage from good to really great. I know these strategies work because they are based on a winning combination of sound research, common sense, and experience. They also work because they approach the most basic aspects of your marriage in unexpected ways. It is the *presence* of these strategies and new behaviors in your marriage that will lead to an exceptional relationship with your spouse. I am confident that these small changes in behavior and attitudes will produce significant, positive benefits to your marriage.

You may have noticed that all four steps so far concentrate

on the exciting, fun, and positive behaviors or attitudes that you can easily adopt and weave into your married life. These steps to making your marriage great are all about *adding* specific positive and rewarding experiences to your relationship. I have shown you how to achieve: (1) realistic expectations of your relationship and spouse; (2) affective affirmation and support; (3) daily briefings to get to know your partner; and (4) change that reduces marital boredom and keeps the relationship fresh.

Now, what about the problematic or bothersome things that occur in your relationship—*things you'd love to get rid of but don't know how to?* The fifth step to making your marriage really great is to reduce costly behaviors. Doing so tips the emotional scale—the overall way you and your spouse feel about your marriage—so the relationship feels profitable for both partners and vastly more rewarding. The *absence* of these troubles or complaints is as important for nurturing a happy marriage as the presence of the rewarding behaviors and attitudes you've learned so far.

In Step 5 you will learn effective strategies to defray the problematic behaviors in your relationship. Once you apply them, the negative costs will go down and the positive benefits will gain momentum. The essential point to understand is that you need to weed out the problematic behaviors in your relationship if you want the positive and rewarding behaviors you learned in Steps 1 through 4 to continue to give you happiness over time. If not, the costly behaviors will tip the balance of your relationship in a negative way and stand in the way of happiness for both you and your partner.

In this chapter, I focus on the six behaviors that are most

likely to tip your relationship happiness toward the deficit side of the balance sheet. I also offer practical and concrete ways to move around these obstacles so you can enjoy the benefits of your marriage. I have found that couples who define themselves as "happy" have been able to reduce the frequency of costly or problematic behaviors so that the positives outweigh the negatives in their marriage.

RELATIONSHIP COSTS

In this fifth step, I am asking you to identify the costly behaviors in your marriage and strategize ways to eliminate or change them. A relationship cost is a behavior your partner does that is a recurrent source of irritation to you. Perhaps it bugs you that your spouse is perpetually late to everything, including picking up the kids from school. Or that your partner always puts his dishes in the sink without cleaning them or stacking them in the dishwasher. A relationship cost can also be a problem or issue that never gets resolved or settled in your marriage, which creates persistent tension or conflict for the two of you. A classic example I see time and again when I work with couples is when the husband and wife can't seem to resolve their differences regarding how to discipline and raise their children. Every time the issue comes up, they blow up and yell at each other. Another common topic that creates tension is when spouses cannot settle differences around their respective extended families—how much time to spend with them, how to share time with both sides of the family, how much information to disclose, and the like.

The presence of costly behaviors makes you and your spouse angry, upset, and irritated. Also, these negatives tend to add up over time. As these issues accumulate and become habitual, they detract from the presence of positive and rewarding behaviors and experiences in your marriage. This gets translated into a feeling of discontentment or unhappiness. The good news is that when you add positive behaviors and subtract negative ones, happiness increases. You probably already know, intuitively, which behaviors in your marriage feel costly and somewhat detrimental.

Can you make issues like these go away? No, of course not. They are part of life. What I'm suggesting is that our *reactions* to life's challenges—not the challenges themselves—are what become costly behaviors. I am going to show you how to change your behaviors around these inevitable hurdles so you can sail right over them and get to the good stuff in your marriage.

AUDIT YOUR RELATIONSHIP

Think hard about what might be the costly behaviors in your marriage. Every couple has them. If you have difficulty coming up with the problems in your relationship, try keeping a daily journal of each interaction (face-to-face, phone, email, text) you have with your spouse. This journal should briefly describe the communication, whether you experienced a positive or negative feeling during or after the communication, and what specific events or actions precipitated this emotion. Write down these feelings and events for four days. Once you identify the costly behaviors, the ones that created negative feelings within you, you can start weeding them out of your relationship.

Psychologists have developed a theory that people keep track mentally of how much emotional currency they spend in a love relationship compared with how much they earn or get back, much like a tax audit. You've probably done this yourself in the past with ex-lovers. "He's just not worth the effort," you might have said to yourself, or "I don't get much back from her—it's give, give, give." You do the same in your marriage, whether you are aware of it or not. You evaluate your relationship based on the rewards versus costs.

Rewards are the relationship experiences or partner behaviors that are positive, uplifting, and joyful (e.g., he gives me affective affirmation, she really knows and understands me, she supports me in times of trouble or stress, he makes my life interesting and exciting, our sex life is very satisfying). *Costs* are the experiences or partner behaviors that trouble you or give you displeasure (e.g., she doesn't get along with my family, he withholds information about finances from me, we can't discuss his past). In most cases, these rewards and costs aren't items you check off on a balance sheet literally. Instead, you keep sort of a ledger or tally in your head of everything that is happening. You then evaluate your mental list of positive and negative experiences. The outcome of your evaluation determines whether you are really happy.

Here is the big idea. If the costs of being in your marriage are greater than the benefits you derive from the relationship, you will describe yourself as unhappy. But when the irritating experiences and issues in your relationship decrease and the positive, rewarding experiences increase, you will feel happy. In my marriage study, we ask the couples to describe their marriages and how they feel about them. The ones who report being "happy" or "very happy" all have one thing in common: No matter what tragedies or challenges they have gone through, the positives outweigh the negatives in their marriages.

Remember, this doesn't mean that you can't experience any negatives or complaints. But picture a scale and pretend you are weighing the daily interactions that make up your relationship. Put the positive experiences on one end of the scale, and the negative issues or troubles on the other side. If you want to take your relationship to a new level of happiness, the positive side needs to weigh a lot more. In fact, psychologist John Gottman studied couples and found that the rewards or positive experiences need to outweigh the negatives by a specific ratio of five to one, or 83 percent positive to 17 percent negative. In practical terms, that means you want to have five positive experiences in your marriage interactions for every one negative experience you have. When you think about it, this is a scientific formula that you can use to measure happiness in your marriage. But rather than get caught up in math and calculations, your goal should be to make sure the rewards in your marriage *outweigh* the costs. In my clinical experience, I have found that people intuitively know when there are more rewards than costs in their relationships. We will talk more about how to measure your own relationship costs and rewards using the Cost-Reward Balance Sheet exercise on pages 171–73.

But first, take the example of Guillermo and Magda, a couple in one of my marriage enrichment workshops, who have been together for the past seven years. Yes, they admitted to having conflict over who dominates the TV choices, why he won't go to church with her, and why she spends so much money on clothes. But they also giggle in the morning over coffee, can't wait to share their day's experiences each evening, spend great vacations in the Ozarks every Memorial Day holiday, work out together on Saturday afternoons, and love being with each other. If you asked either one, they would agree that their negative squabbles or relationship costs don't even come close to the frequency of wonderful, positive, and happy times they experience together on a daily basis.

You may want to keep track in your head to see if that five-to-one ratio holds true in your relationship. But don't worry if your positive-to-negative ratio doesn't match what Gottman is suggesting. I am going to provide you with easy, practical ways to deal with the costly behaviors in your marriage so that you can shift the balance in your relationship back to the positive side.

THE COST-REWARD BALANCE SHEET

On the following pages is a list of common costly behaviors, based on the interviews we conducted in my long-term study of married couples, as well as a list of beneficial behaviors happy

COST-REWARD BALANCE SHEET

Read down the left column first (costly behaviors), and check only those behaviors that happened *often* in the past few months of your marriage. *If a behavior only happened once in a while, don't put a check mark beside it.* Next, read down the right-hand column and do the same thing. When you are finished, look at how many check marks you have in the deficits column, compared with how many you have in the rewards column. There is no perfect score, but the idea is that in a happy marriage, you don't want to have too many costly behaviors, and you want to have lots of beneficial behaviors. In other words, your rewards should outweigh your costs. Your spouse can do this exercise too.

Costly Behaviors (Deficits)	✓ Often	Beneficial Behaviors (Rewards)	✓ Often
We bicker and nag at each other.		I tell or show my spouse I value and appreciate something he or she does.	
I am irritated or resentful about what my spouse did or didn't do.		We talk to each other and ask about each other's day.	
I am not completely honest with my spouse about something—money, an activity, etc.		My spouse knows where I am and what I'm doing.	
We argue in such a way that I feel pessimistic about our future prospects.		When we disagree, we find a solution that works for the most part.	

Costly Behaviors (Deficits)	✓ Often	Beneficial Behaviors (Rewards)	✓ Often
My spouse is critical about a friend or family member in a hurtful way.		We mutually steer clear of topics that really make one or both of us crazy.	
I avoid an important topic because I am afraid of the conflict it causes.		I check in with my partner's current stressors and emotional challenges.	
My spouse puts me down when we're around others.		I touch, hug, kiss, and cuddle with my spouse.	
I avoid spending my free time with my spouse.		We make an effort to do something together—go out to dinner, take a walk, watch our favorite TV show, etc.	
I blame my spouse for things I am partly responsible for.		I am supportive toward my spouse.	
I feel unhappy about the quality of our sex life.		We try to keep things equal around the house, and if they aren't, we acknowledge it.	
My spouse flirts or I flirt with others in a way that provokes jealousy.		We consciously do things to keep our life together interesting, changing, and different.	
I avoid discussing my spouse's problems because they feel burdensome.		We miss each other when our lives get too busy and separate.	

Costly Behaviors (Deficits)	✓ Often	Beneficial Behaviors (Rewards)	✓ Often
I ignore or dismiss my spouse when he or she is trying to talk to me.		I enjoy having sex with my spouse.	
I lose my temper with my spouse.		We laugh together and enjoy each other's company.	
The division of labor in our home feels unfair.		I make him or her feel I can be counted on.	

couples typically cited. As an exercise, think back through the past few months of your marriage. Put a check mark beside the behaviors that happened *often*—not just once or twice. The behaviors on the two sides of this balance sheet are not opposites. In other words, it's possible to have a check mark on both the left side *and* the right side in the same row. When you are done, compare the number of check marks in the deficit column on the left with those in the rewards column on the right. If you are very happy in your marriage, the rewards will outnumber the deficits. If you checked a lot of costly behaviors, it may be time for you and your spouse to work on weeding some of them out.

Rhonda and Marcus are a good example of a couple who has learned how to balance the costs and rewards in their relationship.

"We definitely have our differences," says Marcus. "She is one crazy chick after nine at night. A real night owl. I'm winding down watching TV in bed, and she's in the kitchen with heavy metal blasting on the CD player and making fudge. The kitchen looks like a tornado hit it. Guess who cleans up in the morning?" Marcus emphasizes that they have worked out most of their serious differences. His drinking early on in the marriage, for instance, was a major issue for Rhonda, "so I cleaned up my act." On the topic of arguing, Marcus says, "She used to hold on to grudges for days. Now we talk things out." The two discussed money problems and division of household work as their main sources of conflict. But they showed a great deal of affection for each other, both mentioned the comfort they got in their extended families being so involved in their life and that of their son, and both spouses said they were "very happy." Marcus said he was happier now than when they were first married, and Rhonda nodded in agreement.

TOP-SIX COSTLY BEHAVIORS

One important area I examined in my marriage study was what spouses felt were the thorny issues or most common problems in their marriages. My findings suggest that there are six common problems both husbands and wives find irritating in their marriages. Keep in mind as you are reading through the next section that these six issues or complaints are negative experiences or issues that spouses feel are *present* in their marriage. The couples were not asked to report on positive or rewarding experiences that are *absent* in the marriage, which we focused on in Steps 1–4 (i.e., realistic expectations;

affective affirmation and support; emotional intimacy and closeness; freshness, passion, and satisfying sex).

Let's look at the six costly behaviors that the spouses in my study reported as most problematic or troubling to them in their marriages. If any of these behaviors resonate with you or sound very familiar, you will learn simple strategies to effectively reduce each one. The simple act of learning how to deal with the costly behavior can lead to a much more happy and satisfying marriage.

Costly Behavior #1. You and your spouse fight all the time.

Strategy

Fight fair when you have disagreements. Acknowledge that it is okay to have some taboo topics—and then agree to disagree.

Some conflict with your spouse is normal. You and your spouse come from different backgrounds, different families, perhaps even different cultures, religions, and economic classes. And don't forget that you are of two different genders—which we have learned accounts for different perspectives, approaches, and problem-solving styles. How could you expect to agree on everything? Most studies find that it is not conflict in and of itself that is detrimental to your relationship, but the way you handle or resolve your differences. It is essential that you feel you can resolve disagreements, even if you both agree to disagree on certain topics. A common characteristic of unhappy marriages is that chronic disagreements remain unresolved.

The happy couples I have observed over many years have

all learned how to manage conflict in a constructive, rather than destructive, way. Here's what thirty-seven-year-old Roberta, a homemaker and mother of three, had to say about fighting.

> My advice to young couples? Set rules for fighting. Cool off before you say too much, but don't give it too much time because you might not say something you need to. Control your anger. Each should have a say in all important matters. Learn how to compromise. And make sure you listen—really listen—to what your spouse is trying to tell you or is upset about. We really got better at fighting over the years, and I think it's a skill that has kept us sane and happy. We air things out, and we don't let stuff build up.

The way you and your spouse handle or manage conflict when it does arise determines whether it is a costly behavior in your relationship or not. If you consistently handle conflict in a destructive manner—like yelling, interrupting, calling your partner names, or walking out—studies show that one or both spouses is likely to feel unhappy in the marriage. My long-term research overwhelmingly finds that couples who resolve their conflicts in an unhealthy manner are less happy and less likely to stay married. In a good relationship, the two of you can disagree, but you need to do so fairly.

I am reminded of a patient and fellow therapist, Ann, who told me she actually loves to fight with her husband once in a while. "He gets so emotional—we both do," she told me.

"And it gives us a chance to really air things out. We both feel so relieved and happy and in love later." She emphasized that never in their fights does either one give ultimatums. In other words, Ann and her husband feel safe with their emotional honesty, and the fight becomes a vehicle for better understanding and closeness. That is a fantastic model for fair fighting.

THE LOVE DOCTOR'S SIX TIPS FOR FIGHTING FAIR

Here are some tips to help you and your spouse fight fair the next time conflict arises.

1. *It is okay to go to bed mad.* I'm quite serious. It's a myth that going to bed mad is a bad idea. At night you're tired and irrational. Better to sleep on it and promise your spouse that you'll revisit the issue in the light of day, well rested.

2. *Calm yourself with a break.* If your fight isn't at night, it's okay to walk away—as long as you tell your partner that you're going to come back very soon to finish the discussion. Studies show that we're not able to problem solve when we're extremely upset and emotional. The brain needs at least thirty minutes to calm down and return to normal functioning. So, if you are really beside yourself, tell your partner that you want to discuss the issue, but you need to take a forty-five-minute break and will be back.

3. *Find the right time and situation.* It's really important to pick a time to deal with hot-button topics when you can be alone together with no distractions. For instance, make an appointment to talk things out more formally—don't hit your spouse with the problem that has been troubling you as soon as he or she walks in from work. Emailing, texting, IMing, and telephoning are also good ways to *initiate* (although not resolve) prickly conversations. Walking and talking is also a great option—especially for men, who often find communication easier when they are engaged in an activity.

4. *Address specific behaviors.* When you bring up a conflict-riddled topic, be sure you address specific behaviors that annoy you, rather than attacking the other person or his or her personality traits. For example, you should say, "When you throw your clothes on the floor, I get upset because our room feels chaotic to me," rather than, "You are such a slob." Giving your spouse a specific behavior to focus on allows him or her to work on a solution geared specifically to that behavior.

5. *Be prepared to compromise.* If it seems as though you are always giving in to your spouse, make sure there is some reciprocity over the long haul. But in general, compromise. Sometimes do it your way and other times do it your spouse's way. It really is the only way to go. You also can end up with a solution that is somewhere in the middle of both of your strong opinions or views.

6. *Apologize.* Take time to apologize to each other, even if you didn't start the argument. We all make mistakes and

sometimes we need to acknowledge that we had a part in an argument getting out of hand. This often reminds spouses why they care about and love each other. Even if you just say, "I'm sorry we are fighting," you can begin to settle your differences.

Taboo Topics

As anyone in a relationship knows, there are always a few topics that you may not ever be able to resolve with your partner. These are called taboo topics—issues that will never get worked out or that are perpetual sources of conflict. The most common taboo topics in marriages are politics, family, and religion.

Some taboo topics are perfectly fine between couples and do not necessarily say anything about the quality or compatibility of your relationship. It can become a problem, though, if you have too many taboo topics, or if the topics that are unresolved are major and very significant to your day-to-day lives and your future together, such as whether or not to have children, or how to spend or save your money. Sometimes you can work these differences out or reach a compromise. As long as you *both* agree to disagree, this is an effective strategy to deal with this costly behavior. If not, then fighting over this issue becomes a costly behavior, which can tip the scale toward the negative side of your emotional balance sheet and prevent you from enjoying the rewards in your relationship. One or both of you may also begin to resent the other over time. Spouses need to feel that they can work out their problems together.

Once you can diminish chronic fighting and unfair fighting in your marriage, you will both feel happier.

Costly Behavior #2: You and your spouse can't talk with each other anymore. It feels as though everything is misinterpreted or misunderstood.

Strategy

Send clear messages to your partner by learning effective communication skills.

Effective communication and feeling understood by your partner are critical to relationship happiness. Psychologists have found that spouses who communicate poorly with each other are very dissatisfied and unhappy in their relationships. So if you want your spouse to understand you, it is very important that you send clear messages so that he or she really understands you and doesn't misinterpret what you say.

THE LOVE DOCTOR'S DOS AND DON'TS FOR COMMUNICATING CLEARLY

DO: Stay focused on a single issue. This is true for emails too. If you have something important to say to your spouse, figure out the main message and say it clearly. Don't muddle it up with asides and tangential "alsos."

DON'T: Engage in what I call "kitchen-sinking." Kitchen-sinking is when you bring all of the problems or issues that have been accumulating over time into this conversation. What can happen is that you begin with something that aggravated you yesterday, and before you know it you are bringing up the party last week, a nasty habit that has been going on for months, and the way your partner treated your best friend last year at a potluck. If you stay focused on a single issue, it's so much easier for your spouse to understand and talk with you.

DO: Validate your partner's feelings. This lets him or her know that you acknowledge there is another point of view.

DON'T: Dismiss his or her feelings. Stay away from comments like, "That's such a crazy thing to say." Allow your partner to have and own his or her feelings. So you might say, "I know you must be angry about how I reacted to your mother's comments last night. Here's where I was coming from . . ." You don't have to agree with your partner to validate his or her feelings. If you validate rather than dismiss those feelings, it's so much easier for your spouse to hear what you have to say, and the conversation will be much more rewarding.

DO: Keep the conversation nonthreatening.

DON'T: Engage in name calling when you talk to each other. There are always multiple ways of conveying your message to your partner. Start with a positive comment before you get to the hard stuff. Don't put your partner on the defensive, because when people feel threatened they tend to protect themselves by name calling, cursing, and other hurtful knee-jerk reactions. In order to keep costs low and benefits high, remember that you don't want to say something you will regret later on.

DO: Keep the conversation specific.

DON'T: Use statements like "always" and "never." These irrefutable and general comments box your partner in with no way out. In this impossible situation, he or she will usually just withdraw or get more upset.

DO: Be direct and give your spouse a chance to respond in kind.

DON'T: Assume that you understand or can predict your spouse's thoughts and feelings without asking. Always ask. A very common situation I hear about from patients is that they expect their spouses to know when they are upset about something. They assume that after fifteen or so years of being together, their spouses should know when they are upset by looking at their expression, noticing their posture, or sensing their mood change. Don't assume he or she can read you. Instead, if you want your spouse to know you are angry about something, *just say it*. Direct communication is always the best route.

DO: Take responsibility for your feelings and actions when you talk by using "I" statements.

DON'T: Put the blame on your partner for your lack of being understood. Instead of telling your partner, "You made me feel upset," you might say, "I am not comfortable with what happened."

Bear in mind, the costs of not being understood undermine a relationship. It is important that you speak clearly so that your partner can understand you.

Costly Behavior #3: You and your spouse do not manage household responsibilities fairly.

Strategy

Talk to your spouse about how to divide the household tasks more fairly. Fairness, equity, and respect are essential for marital happiness.

Sociological studies find that men are participating in household tasks more than ever before. But every study, including my own, continues to show that women still do the majority of work around the home, even when they are employed outside the house. In fact, I have found from my therapy practice and my research study that management of household responsibilities is one of the areas couples argue about most.

Oftentimes, though, the issue is not about who does the dishes or the laundry. Those are the external symptoms. The underlying issues—and the ones that are more costly from a happiness perspective—are about fairness, equity, respect, and appreciation. Both partners want to feel like a team, and both want kudos for their hard work.

DID YOU KNOW...

When the happy wives in my study were asked, "How much does your husband help in child care responsibilities?" over 78 percent said, "a lot" (compared with only 50 percent of the other wives).

The housework doesn't have to be divided equally. It just has to be divided equitably, as seen by each spouse. In other words, both partners should feel that their share of household responsibilities is fair. Maybe the wife does more of the shopping and cooking, but she is fine with that because her husband brings in more income, and that helps to pay for a weekly cleaning service.

And, of course, the meaning can differ from one couple to another about what that fair division might be. For one couple, it might be seen as fair for the wife to do the laundry, dishes, cooking, cleaning, and child care, while the husband does the grocery shopping, household repair, and yard work. For another couple, fairness is fifty-fifty in all household responsibilities. Sometimes spouses don't think the division of housework is fair, but they do all of the housework anyway because they want to preserve peace in the relationship. They think the other spouse is threatened by housework, or they don't like how their partners perform the tasks.

A patient of mine named Rick was having problems with

his relationship. His wife, Katie, a self-described "super-mom," is a highly energetic business owner, and they have two school-age kids. The problem was that Rick felt ignored in the marriage. When I asked him to describe a typical day, he said, "I come home from work. Katie is doing homework with the kids and fixing dinner. After dinner she spends time getting the kids to bed, and then goes upstairs and either reads or works at her computer." I suggested to Rick that maybe he could get more involved in "her" activities—the housework and the kids. He told me he could cook Italian meals, which he learned from his mother, and he thought he could try that with the family. Rick came back to our session two weeks later and said he had told Katie he wanted to shop and cook once a week so she could have a break. He also said he wanted to take turns putting the kids to bed, which he did. "You'd have thought I gave her a diamond necklace. I can't remember seeing her so happy and grateful! She's been really attentive to me."

Like Rick, you might be wondering why Katie didn't just ask him to take on more housework. Sometimes spouses don't know how to ask, or just don't bother. This is a good lesson (for husbands, in particular) to remember.

For happy couples, both spouses need to feel as though they are working together for the management of the house and that the division of tasks is fair. This is especially important for wives and how they see the marriage. One of the most interesting findings from my study is that when wives perceive equity and fairness in tasks around the home, they are almost *twice* more likely to report being happy and content in

TIP FOR MEN

If you want to get your wife "in the mood," scoot over to the sink after dinner and offer to do the dishes. A March 2008 report published in the *Council on Contemporary Families* found that men who do more housework have more frequent sex.

their marriages than women who perceive the division of household labor as unequal and unfair.

What if you and your spouse do not manage the household responsibilities fairly? If you are a woman and you want your husband to help around the house, you must let him do the chores his way, even if it isn't perfect. If you continue to criticize him for not doing a task well enough or he doesn't do it the way you do, he will lose his motivation and withdraw from you and the relationship. So he uses the wrong-size baggie when he packs the cookies in the kids' lunch bags. It's okay! So he puts the knives in the fork compartment in the drawer when he unloads the dishwasher. It's not the end of the world! And if you expect your husband to remember everything you want him to get at the grocery store without a list, be prepared for some big disagreements. Make a very specific list of the groceries you would like him to buy. Tell him the exact time he needs to pick up your daughter at soccer practice. Write down the specific cold-remedy flavor the kids don't mind taking before he heads out to the drugstore.

On the flip side, if you are a man, remember that you should continue to ask your wife if you can help with household chores, even if she consistently says "No, thank you." The problem or costly behavior arises when you stop asking if you can help, even if she tells you she doesn't need your help. Also, remember that there are many, many tasks around the house. If your wife is doing the laundry or the dishes, make sure you help and perform other tasks such as taking out the garbage, yard work, grocery shopping, or car repairs. Since divvying up household chores is a hot-button topic for so many couples, I encourage spouses to discuss this issue with each other even before they get married or live together.

Once you start dealing with the costly behavior, you will find that a harmony will settle over your relationship. Each of you will feel like you are part of a winning team, and you'll be able to enjoy the other benefits and positives in your happy relationship.

Costly Behavior #4: You are worried that your partner might be attracted to other people. The green-eyed monster is rearing its ugly head.

Strategy
Build self-confidence and share your concerns with your spouse.

Jealousy is a common experience in romantic relationships. We feel jealous when we're afraid of losing a valued relationship. As you learned in Step 1, it is a myth that jealousy is a sign of extreme love. In fact, jealousy and possessiveness

DID YOU KNOW...

If you think jealousy isn't related to marital happiness, think again. None of the happy couples in my study reported being worried that their spouse was attracted to others, compared to 18 percent of the other couples—who said they "often" or "sometimes" felt worried.

arise from fear and low self-esteem. The experience of feeling jealous says more about your own lack of confidence and insecurities than about the intensity of your love for your partner.

It is important to realize that reactive jealousy—the kind of jealousy you feel in response to an actual threat to the relationship—is not a costly behavior. It is a normal biological response to a condition you perceive as dangerous—the danger of losing your marriage. Suspicious jealousy, on the other hand, is a costly behavior. It occurs when your spouse hasn't actually done anything that sabotages the security of your marriage, and your suspicions do not fit with, or are not warranted by, the facts at hand.

This distinction is important, because everybody feels reactive jealousy when they know their partner has been unfaithful. Suspicious jealousy is the type that can become a very costly behavior in your marriage, because it often results in worried and mistrustful behaviors to confirm suspicions.

The following are some of my strategies or solutions that

take only minutes, but are effective ways to defray the costs that are associated with your feelings of jealousy. Once you start dealing with your jealous feelings or suspicions, you will feel more confident about yourself and your relationship. The benefits in your relationship will gain momentum, allowing your marriage to flourish and your marital happiness to improve.

THE LOVE DOCTOR'S FOUR TIPS TO COMBAT JEALOUSY

1. *Take an honest look at yourself, first.* Look at yourself, just you, apart from your relationship. Do you depend on the relationship to determine how you're feeling about yourself and your self-worth? Begin to spend time with friends and family who think you are great and care about you. Branch out so your identity is not solely tied to being a spouse. Gain some independence from your husband or wife. The more your definition of self is tied to your own accomplishments and experiences apart from the marriage, the less jealousy you will feel in response to a perceived threat. Remember, your self-worth is not related to your partner's fidelity.

2. *Work on building your self-confidence and self-esteem.* Get out into the world. See old friends. Expand your usual routine. Learn Thai cooking. Take up a martial art. Engage in activities that make you feel good about yourself. Master something new. Feelings of inadequacy will only lead to more jealousy.

3. *Don't compare yourself with others.* Sometimes you can become jealous or worried that your partner might be at-

tracted to others, because you are comparing yourself to others around you. Big mistake! When you do this, you can always find something you don't like about yourself. Instead, focus on your strengths, rather than what others possess that you want or envy. Make a list of ten things you like about yourself and carry the list around with you, just in case you need a reminder now and then.

4. *Fess up and put it out there.* As a therapist, I am a big believer in trying to express your concerns and feelings to your spouse, even if it makes you feel vulnerable or not in control of your feelings. We all have those moments. Your spouse should accept that you will have times when you appear weak and need his or her help. Direct communication is the best way to get your concerns or suspicions heard. You might be surprised to find that your spouse helps with the healing. For instance, he may become more aware of how his flirtatious social behavior is affecting you. Or she might realize that checking in from her cellphone more often lets you know where she is, and is very reassuring.

Costly Behavior #5: You keep secrets or withhold information from your spouse.

Strategy

Analyze *why* you are afraid or reluctant to disclose the whole truth. Then address *that* issue. The "secret" will be less important if you do.

DID YOU KNOW...

When the happy couples in my study were asked about whether they felt that their spouses tell them things that are not completely true, their answers differed *significantly* from those of other couples—confirming that honesty plays a crucial role in marital happiness. Consider:

- 78 percent of the happy couples said they "never" feel that their spouses tell them things that are not completely true about money, compared with only 54 percent of the other couples.
- 90 percent of the happy couples said they "never" feel that their spouses tell them things that are not completely true about their past, compared to only 68 percent of the other couples.

Honesty with your spouse builds trust and intimacy—and we all value honesty in our relationships. We also expect that in trusting relationships, both partners are totally honest and open with each other. When one spouse has secrets or withholds information, this behavior violates the expectations of a trusting relationship. Any behavior that violates the expectations of a trusting relationship may be considered a betrayal. Betrayals have a negative effect on a marriage.

What about "editing" for your spouse's own good? It is

fine to protect your partner from some information (a little privacy is not a bad thing), but if you are hiding important matters, the two of you can't grow as a couple.

There is not a lot of difference between lying and withholding information from your spouse. Both are behaviors that go against the expectations of an open and honest relationship. Both are betrayals, and both can become very costly behaviors. In my study, there were two common areas in which spouses weren't completely honest with each other: money matters and information about a spouse's past. If this strikes a chord with you, there is something you can do to weed out this costly behavior.

In order to build trust with your spouse, you need to share personal details and be completely open and honest. If you are hesitant to do so, take a hard look at that, because it will point a way to the solution. Let's say you aren't sure if you're editing or keeping something a secret. Ask yourself three important questions. First, how do you think your spouse would see the withholding of the information? Would your spouse say it is no big deal? Second, what if your partner withheld the same information from you? How would you feel? Would you feel hurt because there was a lack of trust or openness? Or would you think this was a small and unimportant issue so you would be fine with not knowing? Third, why were you not completely honest with your spouse? Did you feel guilty or fear his or her reaction?

Most people know with 100-percent certainty, when they look at the issue head-on like this, whether they are being honest with their spouses. I recommend to my patients who harbor little or big secrets to make an appointment with their spouses to discuss, first, their fear, guilt, or hesitance about disclosing the information, and second, the information itself. Often, once two partners have talked about the *why* of the secret, the *what* is not really important anymore.

Chantal and Shawn are one of the happy couples from my study who faced a serious challenge in their relationship caused by a secret Shawn had kept from Chantal. Here is her story:

> For the first four years of our marriage, Shawn never told me about the son he had with a former girlfriend. I think he felt shame, and I think he figured I'd be furious—especially because we met when we were so young. I kind of thought I was his one and only. I knew he was hiding something—you always do—but I thought it was about money. It kind of *was* about money, as it turned out. We got a letter from the state child support authorities tracking him down and that's how I found out. I guess the mother had decided enough was enough, and wanted Shawn to help her support their son. I was furious—mostly because he had been lying to me for four years. It's a long story, but I guess you could say it had a happy ending. The boy is in his life now, and I was really angrier that he kept it a secret from me than about anything else. I said, "Shawn, I will always be on your side—as long as you tell me the whole truth. There's nothing worse than lies. I can take any truth—even something as big as someone else's child. But secrets? I can't handle that."

DID YOU KNOW...

Self-disclosure in a relationship is usually reciprocal. There is a widely accepted rule, a kind of unspoken assumption, that if one person discloses something extremely personal, then the other *should* respond at the same level of intimacy. So if you don't want your spouse to have secrets from you, then you need to self-disclose and not keep secrets from him or her. Relationship researchers call this the "norm of reciprocity in disclosure."

Watch what happens in your marriage when you are able to be entirely honest. It is so liberating and rewarding, as Shawn discovered in this last story. Studies show that when self-disclosure, or sharing of personal information, flows freely between two partners, it can create a feeling of deep emotional intimacy or closeness. It is no surprise, then, that the happy couples in my study reported that they did not have secrets from each other—nor did they feel the need to have them.

Costly Behavior #6: You don't get along with your spouse's family.

Strategy

Think of it as a necessary aspect of marriage upkeep—and perform it as a gesture of support.

DID YOU KNOW...

Establishing a good rapport with your in-laws is beneficial to newlyweds and associated with their marital satisfaction. This is according to University of Denver associate professor Mary Claire Morr Serewicz, who studied newlyweds and their in-laws and found that a good relationship with in-laws has a positive impact on the happiness of newly married couples, and a negative relationship with in-laws can lead to marital unhappiness early in marriages.

A common complaint of many couples is that one spouse doesn't get along with the other's family. Sometimes this relationship is fragile because of small things like a needy mother-in-law who constantly pleads to go shopping with her daughter-in-law, or a father-in-law not recognizing that his son-in-law doesn't want him to always pay the restaurant bill. At other times, however, there can be quite a bit of tension and conflict between a spouse and the in-laws. And at these times, this tension surrounds bigger issues, like your spouse's family feeding your kids meat when you have decided as a family to be vegetarian, or a mother-in-law preaching to her daughter-in-law about how to care for a newborn child or cook better food. The issues can build up and be quite problematic to a couple trying to establish their own relationship.

Relationship researchers have found that there are three stages of a marriage when the relationship with a spouse's family can be the most stressful: (1) when couples first get married and families are trying to intermingle, (2) when couples have their first child, and (3) when an in-law or family member becomes seriously ill or needs to be taken care of. You may feel that you just can't meet the expectations of his or her family, while at the same time wanting to be accepted by them. Any differences between family backgrounds become more apparent at these three stages as well.

Although in-law relationships can be very stressful and challenging, when a spouse doesn't get along with his or her partner's family, it is detrimental to the happiness in the marriage. It is critical to learn effective strategies to get along with your in-laws. Bear in mind that you just need to get along with them, not love them like your best friends. For the happy couples in my study, both wives and husbands got along (or at least felt close) with their in-laws. It was important for each spouse to make an effort and try to bridge a relationship with the other partner's family.

Here's what Steve, one of the happy spouses from my study, had to say about family obligations.

Trish made it very clear to me early on that her family was a big part of her life. There was only one problem: I couldn't *stand* her parents. Her father was uptight and really difficult to have a conversation with. Very cold and conservative. Her mom was just the opposite: smothering, I'd call it. Phoning every day, dropping by with groceries, giving me suggestions about how to organize our garage. I mean, the woman didn't stop. At one point, I told Trish I wanted to start skipping family meals and holidays. That made her very unhappy. We came up with a compromise—see her folks a little less regularly. Also, sometimes she went to their house with the kids, but without me. And I made a mammoth effort to be civil—for Trish's sake. And you know, the old folks have kind of grown on me. I can tolerate them okay now and it has brought peace back into our household. They're not going to live forever, and it makes Trish happy that I'm part of her extended-family life. I guess I do it for her. And that's fine.

If, like Steve, you have issues with your spouse's family, there are some straightforward ways you can remedy the situation and eliminate behaviors and attitudes that are costly to your marriage. Here are some simple but effective tips on how to get along better with your in-laws that I have used with couples in my practice and workshops many times.

THE LOVE DOCTOR'S SEVEN TIPS FOR GETTING ALONG WITH YOUR SPOUSE'S FAMILY

1. *Set realistic expectations.* For example, try to accept that in most circumstances the relationship between a mother-in-law and a daughter-in-law will not be as close as that of the relationship between a mother and a daughter. Be gracious and open—that's the best defense against getting hurt feelings. Realistic expectations for this relationship, similar to what you learned in Step 1, reduce frustration.

You always get more out of a relationship when you expect less.

2. *Recognize it for what it is: a control issue.* Usually, the most prickly issue across families is who will have the most influence and power. Parents are fearful of losing total control over their son or daughter. They also don't want to recognize that they are getting older themselves—and therefore losing their power. Once you understand and acknowledge this, dealing with your spouse's family and their control issues will be easier. Let them know, gently, that this is the way you like to manage your children or household. Stay open to the fact that they are older than you and maybe even wiser in some areas.

3. *Validate their differences.* There will often be differences between you and your spouse's family. Don't try to change them. Instead, respect and validate one another's differences. Each of you was born in a different time period, with different values and ways of living. You don't have to agree with each other. Just acknowledge their thoughts and feelings—and hopefully they will follow your lead. The reality is you may not receive respect and validation in return. But bear in mind, as I often tell my patients, each time you disagree: These are the people who raised your spouse to be the special person he or she has become. The relationship isn't always easy, but try to appreciate that fact, even if you don't get along with them personally.

4. *Treat them as honored guests.* Everyone needs to feel special and important. Do your best to help your spouse's family members feel that way. If a stranger came to your house,

you would probably offer him a cup of coffee, and you might sit down and ask him questions about his life. Extend that same type of courtesy to your in-laws. Making even a modest effort with in-laws can have the effect of immediately relieving relationship strain between you and your spouse.

5. *Learn to say when.* Many spouses bang their heads against a wall trying—often without success—to get their partners' families to like and accept them. "If I keep calling her and being generous," the reasoning goes, "my sister-in-law is bound to soften up and start being nice to me." Maybe not. You may need to accept the chill between you and an in-law, and simply learn to be decent and get along. Endless giving without reciprocity is not healthy for you or your marriage.

6. *Maintain your relationship privacy.* Meddling in-laws sometimes want to invade the privacy between you and your spouse. It is vital for your marriage that you set clear boundaries regarding what you tell your in-laws. Don't spill your guts to them about everything. And my number-one rule: Don't disclose information to them about your marriage or spouse. Respect each other's privacy. In return, set limits for what you ask them about. Don't take it personally when they don't want to share their concerns or issues with you.

7. *Ask your spouse for help.* Sometimes your spouse needs to step in and help you. If you have tried to communicate directly with your in-laws, changed your expectations, and been able to say "no" or set boundaries, and there is still a

lot of tension, it might be time to ask your spouse to step in. Your spouse can talk to his or her parents alone or come to your rescue when you are in your in-laws' company. This will not be easy for your spouse, and it will take some time, because parents tend to push our buttons. A husband, for example, might have to say, "Mom, this is how my wife feels about this issue. Please respect her. It is important to me that you get along with each other."

STEP 5 TAKE-AWAYS

In Step 5, I asked you to think about the costly behaviors in your marriage—those problematic, troublesome attitudes and interactions with your spouse that get in the way of happiness. You learned that by weeding out the most unprofitable behaviors using simple strategies, it is possible to tip the scale away from negative experiences toward more positive, rewarding ones. Here is a review of other insights from Step 5:

- The happy couples I have observed in my marriage study report the presence of many positive, rewarding experiences, and the absence of most negative, costly behaviors.
- Rewarding behaviors are all the ones you learned in Steps 1 through 4—positive behaviors that enrich and enhance the relationship and lead to more happiness. Costly behaviors are those that make spouses feel unhappy—such as chronic squabbling, poor communication, small and large betrayals, and disrespectful or hurtful habits.

- To be truly happy in a marriage, your rewarding experiences should outnumber your costly experiences.

- The best way to tip the balance toward more rewarding experiences is to audit your relationship. Identify the behaviors that make you feel unhappy so you can weed out the most unprofitable ones.

- In my long-term study of marriage, there are six behaviors that couples report as being most problematic and costly in terms of marital happiness. They are: chronic unfair fighting; poor communication; an unfair division of household labor and responsibilities; jealousy or power imbalances; secretive or untrustworthy behavior; and conflicts with each other's family.

- For every costly behavior, there are simple strategies you can apply to diminish its impact or eliminate it altogether.

- If you can implement the rewarding behaviors from Steps 1 through 4, and weed out the most unprofitable ones by using the strategies in Step 5, you will be able to take your marriage from good to really great.

CONCLUSION

Seize the moment to make
your marriage exceptional.

s a relationship research scientist, I have had the privilege to delve deeply into the study of marriage, observing and interviewing 373 married couples from the time they first tied the knot, through two decades of their lives, and up to the present. This long-term marriage study has yielded rich insights into how different couples navigate through life and find happiness with their partners. It's been exciting to identify at last what makes couples happy, what a truly great marriage looks like, and most important, how to get there.

We covered a lot of ground in this book. First and foremost, my research shows that, contrary to popular myths about marriage and divorce, *frustration* is the leading reason marriages are unhappy. Having realistic expectations and knowing your husband's or wife's expectations keeps frustration in check, and leads to marital happiness. I also found that in happy marriages, wives and husbands give affective affirmation to each other frequently and feel their spouse is supportive and reliable in a pinch. The happy couples from my study communicate with each other frequently and get to know each other's worlds, friends, dreams, opinions, and values well—but are routinely checking in and being inquisitive about their spouses. In happy marriages I observed, spouses feel surprised and entertained by each other; they make an effort to keep their relationship fresh, alive, sexually satisfying, and not boring. Finally, all of the happy couples seem to have figured out ways to cope with the costliest behaviors or issues—such as fighting, division of household labor, or friction with extended family—so that the positive, rewarding experiences of married life outweigh the negative, costly ones.

From these observations, and from the successes I have seen in my couples therapy practice, I can confidently say that when you introduce realistic expectations, appreciation and support, daily communication that helps you get to know each other, and new and exciting activities—Pow!—you get a really happy marriage. Keep your focus on adding positive elements into your marriage and you'll end up happier and better off than if you merely focus on fixing the problems.

THE SCIENCE BEHIND HAPPY COUPLES

Let's review the big findings from my long-term marriage study in terms of each gender—the ingredients of a happy marriage, if you will.

What Husbands Need

One of the first and most astonishing findings from my NIH research was that the presence of affective affirmation plays a major role in husbands' happiness over time. Men need to receive regular affective affirmation from their wives. When men don't get this, they become distressed and unhappy in the marriage. In Step 2, I showed women how easy it is to give affective affirmation, and I suggested many different ways to do it. I emphasize once again that this single, small behavioral change will make a tremendous difference in your marriage and the way your husband feels and responds. Affective affirmation is one of the most powerful tools wives especially can use to improve the marriage. It is one of the quickest ways to dramatically change the "mood" of the marriage and quality of the dynamic between husbands and wives.

I also found that husbands need to feel they can count on their wives. They list instrumental support—the type of support where you help him work through a problem or challenge—as one of their key requirements for happiness in a marriage. Husbands *don't* want a lot of relationship talk, however. I discovered that frequent relationship talk had a *negative* impact on happiness for men.

Finally, husbands need to enjoy the sexual part of the relationship. Although I found that the frequency of sex declines over time in marriages—even in very happy marriages—the *quality* of sex remained high. Husbands who are in happy marriages report that sex with their wives is good and that it's an important component of their happiness.

What Wives Need

Women have stronger negative associations with conflict than their male counterparts. To be happy in their marriages, wives need to feel that conflict is minimal and manageable. They also love to talk about their emotions and about the relationship. For wives, touching base with their husbands regularly about issues in the marriage is an important determinant of their present and future happiness.

Just as husbands need enjoyable sex to feel happy, wives need emotional connection. They can get it from sex, but they also get it from intimate talk with their husband. Wives who report high levels of happiness over time feel a close emotional bond and connection with their spouse.

Finally, an important factor in wives' happiness is to feel the division of household labor is fair. Remember, it isn't really about the actual tasks per se, but more about issues of fairness, respect, and being part of a teamlike approach. So that doesn't necessarily mean all chores are divided fifty-fifty between husband and wife; it just means that the division of labor *feels* fair in the way the two spouses have worked it out. When the division of household responsibilities does not feel fair for wives, happiness decreases over time in their marriage.

What Happy Marriages Need

My research found that *frustration* is the leading reason marriages are unhappy. It's not money or infidelity or other issues from soap opera lore. Frustration grows and festers when couples have unrealistic expectations of marriage and their spouse. Unrealistic expectations lead to frustration, and then happiness begins to erode. In happy couples, husbands and wives have *realistic* expectations of their spouses and marriages. Importantly, in happy marriages, the spouses also *know* what their partners expect. Having realistic expectations and knowing your husband's or wife's expectations keeps frustration in check, and leads to marital happiness.

Being in a relationship rut, or being bored with each other and the marriage, was predictive of marriage unhappiness over time for both husbands and wives. In the happy couples I studied, the spouses described each other as interesting and fun. To keep your marriage happy, bring a steady supply of newness, surprises, and fresh experiences into the relationship and your own individual lives. Slow down your busy life once a day and pay attention to your spouse. This will keep your spouse happy and prevent both of you from getting bored.

I also found that a good connection with your spouse's family is predictive of marital happiness, for both wives and husbands. So build a network of caring and consideration—if not love—for your spouse's siblings, parents, children from previous marriages, and other family members. This has been shown to be a significant, positive factor in happy, strong marriages.

Wives and husbands in happy marriages report that the level of companionate love increases over time. They become better friends and they have lots to talk about. Make it a point to talk to your spouse every day about something of importance to him or her. Ask your spouse personal questions that require thought and provoke discussion. Know what stressors your spouse is up against, who your spouse interacts with, and what his or her life goals and dreams are. Doing this regularly will help you get to know each other better and will deepen your friendship and bond, a major factor in happy marriages.

Increase positive experiences; decrease negative ones. The happy couples in my study were like all couples—they too argued sometimes and got on each other's nerves. But the positive experiences far outweighed the negative ones in their marriage. Audit your relationship behaviors often, just as you balance your checkbook, to make sure the rewards outnumber the costs.

Finally, for all happy couples, I found that trust—knowing your partner would not hurt or deceive you—is a major factor in marital happiness. If you want to be happy, you need to be honest with your spouse. This means not lying, but it also means being forthcoming and open. You both need to feel that the relationship is a safe place where you can be vulnerable and fully present. That means bringing up personal, embarrassing, or even potentially contentious topics. Happy couples talk, they share, and they accept their partners.

THE LOVE DOCTOR'S SIX MOTIVATIONAL SECRETS TO HELP YOU ON YOUR JOURNEY

In this book I have not talked about the couples from my study of marriage who divorced or the ones who are chronically unhappy, yet remain together. From observing these unhappy couples, however, I can conclude that relationship unhappiness occurs when one or both partners lack the will, the ability, or the skills to resolve differences and work through challenges together.

But that's not you. You already have the will to make your marriage better. You picked up this book because you are searching for ideas, solutions, and maybe some inspiration that can help you and your spouse take your marriage to a new and different level. You also have the ability to make your marriage better. The happy couples in my study are proof that it doesn't take a lot of money, years of therapy, or a college education to grow, change, improve, and maintain a marriage that is healthy, alive, and strong. As for the skill part of the equation, this book provides you with lots of science-based, concrete tools you can apply right away to improve your marriage. With will, ability, and skills, you have what it takes to boost your already good marriage to a new, fantastic, fulfilling level of greatness.

Now all you need is a little bit of coaching and motivation. I'm going to leave you with a handful of secrets that will help you implement the five steps and stay upbeat and energized on your journey. Whenever you start to feel stuck or maybe a bit discouraged, return to the following six secrets—which

SOME OTHER IMPORTANT FINDINGS AT A GLANCE

Many of the findings from my ongoing long-term study of marriage were shared in this book, along with their implications for happy couples and how they might apply to your own marriage. The project continues to make new discoveries and uncover important information about happy and stable marriages over time. But there are numerous findings about happy, stable couples that I did not include in the chapters, yet are important and interesting nevertheless. Here are just a few of them. See how many apply to your marriage and what kind of conclusions you might draw from them.

• Making communal collaborative concerns a priority over private psychological concerns is a critical task in early marriage that determines how well couples are able to blend lives and achieve happiness.

• When couples continue to characterize their marriage in an overly romantic way years after the "honeymoon period" is over, they are less happy and less likely to manage stressful challenges in their future together than couples who take a more pragmatic view of their married life together.

• Working spouses who are happy with their work are also very happy in marriage. Although other researchers have found that a negative spillover of work distress adds to marital stress, this study is the first to emphasize the *positive* spillover from work to marriage.

• Income or class is not related to marital happiness. Instead, the more financial stress (the stress you experience when you think about your expenses and debts, given your financial situation) that couples experience, the less happiness they report. Couples can experience financial stress or strain at all levels of income or class.

- Spouses whose parents divorced before the spouses had turned sixteen were no more likely to divorce than those spouses whose parents stayed married. Marital happiness does not differ for those spouses whose parents divorced versus spouses whose parents stayed married.

- Couples who lived together before marriage do not differ in happiness from those couples who did not live together.

- Couples are more likely to be happy and less likely to divorce when wives are educated.

- Couples are less likely to divorce when wives attend religious services and activities often.

- In happily married couples, husbands' views of self change over time. Husbands' perceptions of self become more like what their wives perceive them to be.

- In the study, couples are asked to jointly tell the story of their relationship, from when they first met, became a couple, and got married. In happily married couples, spouses easily agree and coordinate their stories, they develop a "we" orientation to their storytelling, and the story content is not particularly romantic, emotional, or dramatic in tone.

- Courtship stories that continue to be romantic and full of emotion over the years are indicators of unhappiness for wives. Clear, detailed, well-crafted stories of the wedding and honeymoon over the years are also predictive of unhappiness for wives. Happier wives, on the other hand, maintain an overall sense of positive affect about the wedding and honeymoon, but they tend to have lost the details.

- Black and white married couples are similar in many ways, but there also are important differences. Four important ones are:

    1) *Couple happiness and likelihood of divorce.* White couples are happier in their marriages, and less likely to divorce, than black couples.

    2) *Egalitarian in beliefs and behaviors.* Black couples are more egalitarian in their beliefs and behaviors than white couples. We found that black husbands are more likely to perform household tasks and child care than white husbands.

    3) *Family ties.* Black couples are less likely to argue over matters pertaining to family, and they visit their family more often than white couples. Also, the close bonds with family and in-laws are more critical to the happiness of black couples than white couples.

    4) *Interdependence.* Being interdependent or intertwined (socially, emotionally, and financially) is more critical to the happiness of white couples than black couples.

are really principles to live your marriage by—to get you back on a positive track.

1. Sweat the Small Stuff.

Most of your adult life, you have heard the opposite. But to maintain a happy marriage, you need to pay attention to the small stuff, the daily obstacles and bumps in the road. My research confirms that deaths, major illnesses, or tragedies such as fire or bankruptcy are not the greatest causes of marital strife and struggle. Interestingly, in times of great hardship, couples tend to lean on each other. When there is great stress coming from outside the marriage, most spouses turn inward for relief, love, and support. They frequently say tough times and life-changing challenges brought them closer together and made their bond stronger.

No, it's not the big events that make couples unhappy but instead the seemingly minor, everyday challenges. Your partner doesn't notice you. Your partner isn't excited by you. Your partner doesn't listen. Your partner seems bored. You snap at each other. There are little squabbles. You get on each other's nerves. Your day-to-day interactions have fallen into an unpleasant pattern, and you just don't feel ecstatic about your relationship. The marriage feels blah and bland.

My big message for you is this: Everyday challenges require—and are easily met by—simple solutions. Don't let the little stuff in your marriage slide or build up. Don't let the minor issues go unaddressed and erode your happiness. Instead, go back and apply my five easy steps so you can change the dynamic between you and your spouse right away.

Another aspect of the "sweat the small stuff" secret is setting short-term, small, achievable goals. Look for brief moments of connection. Share a spontaneous laugh with your wife. Swing your husband around and plant a *real* kiss on his smacker. These are examples of small experiences or goals you can accomplish easily. Psychologists know that success is motivating and leads to real behavioral change when it is repeated. When you set a small goal and then succeed at it, you will be motivated to pursue the next small change, and so on. If there's a large goal you would like to achieve in your marriage, break it down into tiny components—daily behaviors that add up to big change over time—and work on accomplishing these instead.

2. Lighten Up.

One of the qualities I have observed over and over among the happy couples in my marriage study is the ease with which they relate. They joke. They shrug their shoulders with a smile. They are accepting. And they are calm. When things are working well in your marriage, *it's easy*. Don't misunderstand me, happy couples still work on their relationships, but they just don't struggle as much.

If you are working terrifically hard to make things better in your marriage, the last thing you should do is stress out, dig your heels in, and resolve to work harder. Instead, take a step back and see if there's an easier way to do it. It sounds counterintuitive, but it works. How do you move a pile of boulders in the middle of the road? One single rock at a time. The same is true in marriages. When two spouses are able to make mountains *into* molehills, maintaining the partnership doesn't feel like hard work. That is the reason I wrote this book: to tell couples that simple, small behavioral changes can really transform your marriage. It's not hard work, it's easy work!

Pay attention to your spouse. Show her some affection. Surprise him with a small endearment. Listen instead of reacting. Ask a good question. Do a small act that shows support. Above all, don't forget the laughter and delight you had when you were first together. Remember to have fun. Bring a little bit of mirth, lightness, and fresh air into the marriage. The happy marriages I have observed over the years have this element in common: Both spouses contribute to the well-being of the marriage regularly in small but significant ways. They do it without a lot of effort, and they do it often. They do not forget to show each other that they love each other. That's because loving each other has become easy and natural for them.

3. Focus on New, Positive Elements.

The strategies in my book concentrate on bringing new, positive elements into your marriage in order to boost marital happiness. This is a brand-new approach that is in stark contrast to how most relationship experts and marriage counselors address marriage. Other experts advise couples to start with the question, "What's *wrong*?" They look at fighting or sexual problems. They zoom in on the negative aspects of the marriage in an attempt to improve the relationship.

But from my work with couples, I have come to believe strongly that introducing positive behaviors into the marriage is a far more effective way to produce meaningful and lasting change. Why? Because positive changes make us feel good and motivate us to keep going in the same direction. And of course, as we learned in Step 5, as you focus on these rewarding and beneficial experiences in your marriage and keep adding new ones, you also need to effectively manage or reduce the costly or negative behaviors present in your marriage. It is essential to minimize negative experiences in your marriage to keep the frequency of positive experiences high, and the frequency of negative experiences low. But overall, if you have a decent marriage to begin with, it is so much easier and more effective to focus on making small, positive behavioral changes. You will see quick and satisfying results using my approach, and I think you'll find it very energizing.

4. Be an Inspiration to Your Spouse.

When we are having marital problems, we tend to blame our partner instead of taking responsibility for our own part in the problem. Or we try to change our spouse by telling him or her what to do. Both of these tactics will only create resentment. There's a better way to get your spouse moving with you in a new direction: Start with yourself, and that will inspire him or her to do the same.

When a couple comes to therapy for help with their relationship, there is usually one spouse who recognizes things could be better, and often the other one has come along to appease his or her partner. That's okay, and it may even describe you. You are not satisfied with the status quo in your marriage, and would like to see your partnership reach its full potential—greatness. But how do you get your partner to work toward the same objective?

Here's how. First, take responsibility for your own behaviors, actions, and words. You will be surprised at the powerful effect this has on your spouse. When you listen instead of reacting, are considerate instead of self-involved, take time for your spouse instead of marching through a routine, take the initiative on a project instead of waiting for him or her to do it—these are all examples of conscious ways you are changing your routine behavior. Watch what happens: Your spouse will respond in kind.

The key to working together on improving your marriage is to be a team. In any high-functioning team, when one member contributes, other members reciprocate. Psychologists understand that good marriages are based on give and take. It is natural that when one partner gives, the other will reciprocate. Although you may think you have to teach your spouse to give back, trust me, you don't. You don't have to push or nag him or her, either. All you have to do is consciously and consistently pay attention to your *own* behavior. When you do, you will inspire and motivate your spouse to do the same.

5. Empathize.

Try to understand your partner's perspective or frame of mind. When your partner isn't talking, isn't in a good mood, isn't perky, 90 percent of the time *it has nothing to do with you.* Don't take it personally; don't tell yourself that he or she must be reacting to something you've done. Instead, try to put yourself in your partner's shoes—as a woman, a mother, a man, a father, a stressed-out employee—and attempt to understand your spouse's perspective. Try to listen, and look for signals or cues that show you what is going on. Ask questions.

With my college students, I do an exercise to teach them what empathy *feels* like. I tell them: Pretend you wake up one day in the body of the opposite gender. For the next twenty-four hours, your brain and the rest of your body will be that of the other sex. I tell them to write down how they feel, what they would do, how they might react to things, and what type of interactions they might have. At the end of the exercise, I collect their notes and we discuss gender differences, our assumptions about the other gender, and what we have learned about empathy.

You can run through a version of this same exercise in your mind. What is it like to be your spouse? What would it feel like to hear the words you just spoke to him or her? What do your spouse's stressors feel like? In other words, look at life through his or her eyes. Understand that your spouse behaves the way that he or she does because of his or her own baggage, background, and personality.

This guiding principle—being empathetic—will save you so much time, energy, and unnecessary strain in your marriage, and will make other kinds of changes in your relationship a lot easier to accomplish.

6. Seize the Moment.

The final message I want to impart is *seize the moment.* I have seen too many couples, separately or together, who describe their marriage as decent, okay, or just so-so. Nothing is terribly wrong. They get along most of the time, and they manage the house, jobs, kids, and extended family competently. They even love and genuinely care about each other. Yet, they wonder if this is as good as it gets. Life seems to be slipping away too quickly, and the marriage isn't all that exciting. Not having a *great* marriage contributes to less overall life satisfaction and a greater likelihood of physical health problems, such as higher blood pressure, hypertension, heart disease, and chronic ulcers.

If this describes you, then *what are you waiting for?* If you already have a good marriage, you are really fortunate, because it's not complicated or difficult to turn a good marriage into an exceptional one. I have observed many couples who are grateful to share their lives with each other every single day—who spend their time together having fun, feeling close and secure, savoring passionate moments and enjoying sex, and becoming deeper, more intimate friends and lovers as time goes on. This could describe you too.

Don't wait to make changes, try new things, and practice

new behaviors in your marriage. If you work through the simple steps in this book and start to apply some of the tips right away—right now, today!—you will see positive changes in your marriage and your spouse immediately. There's nothing more motivating than to witness instant change. More sex. More attention. More kindness. More fun. More connection. *My five simple steps are the way to get there.*

Here's wishing you the best of luck as you traverse your life journey with your spouse. Along the way, remember that maintaining a great marriage should not feel like hard work. All it takes are simple behavioral changes to make your marriage great. Seize the moment right now to make your marriage exceptional.

BIBLIOGRAPHY

CHAPTER ONE

1. Luo, S., and Klohnen, E. C. (2005). Assortative mating and martial quality in newlyweds: A couple-centered approach. *Journal of Personality and Social Psychology, 88,* 304–326.
2. Sprecher, S., and Metts, S. (1989). Development of the "Romantic Beliefs Scale" and the examination of the effects of gender and gender-role orientation. *Journal of Social and Personal Relationships, 6,* 387–411.
3. Spitze, G., and Loscocco, K. A. (2000). The labor of Sisyphus? Women's and men's reactions to housework. *Social Sciences Quarterly, 81(4),* 1087–1101.
4. Weingarten, H. R., and Douvan, E. (1985). Male and female visions of mediation. *Negotiation Journal, 4,* 349–358.

5. El-Sheikh, M., Buckhalt, J. A., and Reiter, S. L. (2000). Gender-related effects in emotional responding to resolved and unresolved interpersonal conflict. *Journal of Sex Roles, 43(9–10)*, 719–734.

6. Ammon, R. L., and Richard, F. D. (2003). The influence of biology and commitment beliefs on jealousy responses. *The Osprey Journal of Ideas and Inquiry, 4*, 52–70.

7. Shackelford, T. K., Buss, D. M., and Bennett, K. (2002). Forgiveness or breakup: Sex difference in responses to a partner's infidelity. *Cognition and Emotion, 16(2)*, 299–307.

CHAPTER TWO

1. Shackelford, T. K. (2001). Self-esteem in marriage. *Personality and Individual Differences, 30*, 371–390.

2. Murray, S. L., Bellavia, G. M., Rose, P., and Griffin, D. W. (2003). Once hurt, twice hurtful: How perceived regard regulates daily marital interactions. *Journal of Personality and Social Psychology, 84*, 126–147.

3. Falba, T. A., and Sindelar, J. L. (2008). Spousal concordance in health behavior change. *Health Services Research, 43(1)*, 96–116.

4. Cohan, C. L., Booth, A., and Granger, D. A. (2003). Gender moderates the relationship between testosterone and marital interaction. *Journal of Family Psychology, 17(1)*, 29–40.

CHAPTER THREE

1. Wellman, B., Smith, A., Wells, A., and Kennedy, T. (2008). Pew Research Center. Networked families, http://www.pewinternet.org/Reports/2008/Networked-Families.aspx.

2. Pincus, S. H., House, R., Christenson, J., and Adler, L. E. (April–June, 2001). *U.S. Army Medical Department Journal*, 15–23. http://digitallib.amedd.army.mil/cgibin/Pdisplay.cgi/TMP.objres.71.pdf?type=application/pdf&path=/m1/encompass/amed

djlndb/clipboard/.outgoing/TMP.objres.71.pdf&fileaddr=139.161. 100.114&fileport=20132.

3. Wilcox, W. B., and Nock, S. L. (2006). What's love got to do with it? Equality, equity, commitment and women's marital quality. *Social Forces, 84(3)*, 1321–1345.

4. Tannen, D. (1990, 2001). *You Just Don't Understand: Women and Men in Conversation.* New York: HarperCollins.

5. Schramm, D. G., Marshall, J. P. Harris, V. W., and Lee, T. R. (2005). After I do: The newlywed transition. *Marriage and Family Review, 38,* 45–67.

CHAPTER FOUR

1. Tsapelas, I., Aron, A., and Orbuch, T. (2009). Marital boredom now predicts less satisfaction 9 years later. *Psychological Science, 20(5),* 529–533.

2. Berscheid, E., and Walster, E. (1974). A little bit about love. In T. Huston (Ed.), *Foundations of Interpersonal Attraction* (pp. 335–381), New York: Academic Press.

3. Huston, T. L., and Chorost, A. F. (1994). Behavioral buffers on the effect of negativity on marital satisfaction: A longitudinal study. *Personal Relationships, 1,* 223–239.

4. Aron, A., Norman, C. C., Aron, E. N., McKenna, C., and Heyman, R. (2000). Couples' shared participation in novel and arousing activities and experienced relationship quality. *Journal of Personality and Social Psychology, 78,* 273–283.

5. Hughes, S. M., Harrison, M. A., and Gallup, G. G. Jr. (2007). Sex differences in romantic kissing among college students: An evolutionary perspective. *Evolutionary Psychology, 5(3)*, 612–631.

6. Laumann, E. O., Gagnon, J. H., Michael, R. T., and Michaels, S. (1994). *The Social Organization of Sexuality: Sexual Practices in the United States.* Chicago: University of Chicago Press.

7. Wiederman, M. W. (2000). Women's body image self-consciousness

during physical intimacy with a partner. *The Journal of Sex Research, 37,* 60–68.

8. Purine, D. M., and Carey, M. P. (1997). Interpersonal communication and sexual adjustment: The role of understanding and agreement. *Journal of Consulting and Clinical Psychology, 65*(6), 1017–1025.

9. Muller, C., and Thorpe, B. (2008). *365 Nights: A Memoir of Intimacy.* New York: Berkley Trade.

10. Brown, D. (2008). *Just Do It: How One Couple Turned Off the TV and Turned On Their Sex Lives for 101 Days (No Excuses!).* New York: Crown Publishing.

CHAPTER FIVE

1. Gottman, J. M. (2004). *What Predicts Divorce? The Relationship Between Marital Processes and Marital Outcomes.* Hillsdale, NJ: Erlbaum.

2. Coleman, J. (2008). Parents need to get out of the house sometimes, in men's changing contribution to housework and child care, Council on Contemporary Families. http://www.contemporaryfamilies.org/subtemplate.php?t=briefingPapers&extenshousework.

3. Serewicz, M. C. (2008). Toward a triangular theory of the communication and relationships of in-laws: Theoretical proposal and social relations analysis of relational satisfaction and private disclosure in in-law triads. *Journal of Family Communication, 8*(4), 264–292.

ABOUT THE AUTHOR

In addition to her role as the project director of the Early Years of Marriage Project, TERRI L. ORBUCH, PH.D., is research professor at the Institute for Social Research at the University of Michigan and a professor at Oakland University. The host of the weekly The Love Doctor radio show on VoiceAmerica.com, she's been a marriage therapist for more than twenty years. She lives in Michigan with her husband.

www.drterrithelovedoctor.com

ABOUT THE TYPE

This book was set in Granjon, a modern recutting of a typeface produced under the direction of George W. Jones, who based Granjon's design upon the letter forms of Claude Garamond (1480–1561). The name was given to the typeface as a tribute to the typographic designer Robert Granjon.